1 Chapter

INTRODUCTION

1.0 General Introduction:

Education plays a key role in the development of a nation. World over it has been realized that no country can progress without the qualitative development of its human capital. Education plays a key role in the development of human resources. Education is one of the factors affecting the physical and growth of an individual. Today education is seen as a series of teaching, thinking, learning experiences behavior in a specified desired manner. Educational objectives are no longer limited to the three R's - Reading, Writing, and Arithmetic. The educational structure of any country starts with primary education is to be laid at this stage and the teachers at the primary level have pivotal role to play. From the philosopher to the laymen, everyone eulogies the teacher as the mason who builds the fabric of society the students being the bricks and mortar of the future. From the earliest times teachers have had a hazardous and onerous task to perform – to mold the body, mind and soul. A teacher is no longer viewed as the transmitter of knowledge, or dispenser of wisdom, but as a diagnostician, guide, assistance appropriate – encourager, stimulator, promoter and an interactive participant in the education precede teacher walks on a tight rope between the reality of today and the anticipation of tomorrow and the distant future. Therefore, the role of a teacher has to take on new dimensions. National policy of education emphasized mainly on the important of quality of education. One of the factors identified as contributing to the important of quality of education is dedicated teachers, their personality and teaching competency.

1.1 Teachers in the System of Education:

The most important factor that decides the quality of education is the teacher. The teacher is the pivot of any educational system. All committees and commissions have emphasized the importance of the role of the teacher in education. As pointed out by the Secondary Education Commission (1952-53), "Every teacher and educationist of experience knows that even the best curriculum and the most perfect syllabus remains dead, unless quickened into life by right methods of teaching and right kind of teachers". The teacher becomes the cogwheel of the entire educational system; the healthy functioning and success of the system depends upon his strength and ability to innovate methods and media to meet the needs of his class.

As pointed out earlier, the success of education depends up on the standard of teacher. It is generally realized that the teacher plays an important role in education. However good may be the system of education, curricula and textbooks if the teachers are not efficient, education by and large will be ineffective. The education and its contribution to the nation development include the part played by the teachers. The success of education is also based on the personality and competence of the teacher.

1.1.1 Importance of Teachers:

No system of education, no syllabus, no methodology, no textbooks can rise above the level of its teachers. If a country wants to have quality education it must have quality teachers"-V.S Mathews.

National Policy on Education (1986), emphasis the teacher and his/her important role in bringing about desirable changes in education. It says, the government and community should endeavor to create conditions which will help motivate the inspire teachers on constructive and creative lines. Teachers should have the freedom to innovate, to devise appropriate methods of communications and activities relevant to the needs and capabilities of and the concerns of the community.

"A lamp can never light another lamp unless it continues to burn its own flame" -RavindraNath Tagore.

Schools are nurseries of human progress and classrooms shape the destiny of the nation. The position if the teacher is of paramount importance. Besides educational progress, the every existence of the social, economical and political life of country or the continuity of civilization itself in the world depends ultimately upon the work of the teachers in the schools. In the words of Saiyidain (1965), a teacher who has a genuine love for his children and even intelligence and psychological insight may not be able to solve, for love can unlock many doors to which reason may not to be able to find the key. The true teacher must discover the divine spark, however feeble and deeply embedded in the ages, which is to be found in almost every child and cherish it with tender care. The teacher's influence is everlasting. He shapes the testing of future citizens. In shaping a nation there are many kinds of architects who may take part in its construction but none that has a more decisive part to play then the teacher.

1.2 Personality:

In the educational field, that is in the process of teaching – learning process, Personality factors are quite significantly influential. Since teaching learning is a mental process and it involves both the teacher and the learner to be active and the teaching is effective if the teacher assess the Personality of the student. Teacher can change his or her methods or techniques according to the personality of the individual, Personality of an individual are considered to be a combination of different constituents or dimensions.

Some of which we can explicitly observe and measure the physical characteristics such as height , weight , aptitude etc. and other which we cannot measure or observe are feeling, ideas, attitudes, convictions, motives, aspirations, self-concept, and personality.

Personality is, in a sense, self-expression of one to the outer world. An individual starts shaping his personality from birth through his interaction with numerous variables; that is, he lays the foundations of his own life. In our modern social life, a healthy personality development enables the individual to perform his social role effectively, to lead an organized and happy life and to gain a meaning in the society. Schools, a social institution, are the main environmental factors effective in the development of personality. Teachers and parents are the ones who influence the student most. The studies up to now have showed that the personality of a teacher surely affect his TEACHING and students.

Personality can be defined as a dynamic and organized set of characteristics possessed by a person that uniquely influences his or her cognitions, motivations, and behaviors in various situations (Ryckman, 2004). The word "personality" originates from the Greek *persona*, which means mask. Significantly, in the theatre of the ancient Latin-speaking world, the mask was not used as a plot device to *disguise* the identity of a character, but rather was a convention employed to represent that character.

The pioneering American psychologist, Gordon Allport (1937) described two major ways to study personality, the nomothetic and the idiographic. Nomothetic psychology seeks general laws that can be applied to many different people, such as the principle of self-actualization, or the trait of extraversion. Idiographic psychology is an attempt to understand the unique aspects of a particular individual. The study of personality has a rich and varied history in psychology, with an abundance of theoretical traditions. Some psychologists have taken a highly scientific approach, whereas others have focused their attention on theory development. Personality is a determinant of behavior. According to Kurt Lewin's formula:

BEHAVIOR (B) = F [PERSONALITY (P), ENVIRONMENT (E)]

We can see that the determinants (causes) of behavior can be separated into 2 classes of variables: personality and environment. The difference is that personality variables are internal causes of behavior (inside the skin) and environmental variables are external causes of behavior.

Eysenck (1960) defined personality as more or less stable and enduring organization of a person's character and temperament, intellect and physique, which determine his unique adjustment to the environment. Eysenck was able to discover, by means of factor analytic techniques, two fundamental dimensions of personality: Neuroticism and Extroversion –Introversion. One among the version is Maudsley personality inventory. It is concerned with personality traits of the individual. It is designed to measure ones neuroticism and extraversion.

1.2.1 Neuroticism:

Neuroticism refers to a general emotional over responsiveness, emotional liability and liability to neurotic breakdown under stress. High scoring individuals tend to be anxious, worrying and depressed. The neurotic has a tendency to worry over little things to be unable to make up his mind. He feels inadequate to sleep in the night due to tenseness. He has illogical fear and is pursued by trouble some thoughts. A neurotic is needed medical care and treatment.

Neuroticism is a tendency or disposition to develop neuroses. Neuroses are mild mental, nervous disorder; neurotics are in touch with reality. They frequently have anxiety, worry, stress, strain and guilty feelings. They ponder too much about the impending disaster. They have unresolved conflicts, insecurity, obsessive, compulsive's reactions, phobic's and other host of other neurotic disorders.

1.2.2 Extroversion:

According to Eyesenck (1968) extraversion refers to impulsive behavior with sociable tendencies. High scores on extraversion are, indicative of outgoing, impulsive and uninhibited behavior.

Extroversion is characterized as an outward flowing of libido. The extrovert is hearty gregarious there by making friends easily. He has no inhibitions. He takes initiative in the social action. He is materialistic, practical, objective and experimental. He laughs readily. The extravert is dominated and governed by practicality. Persons with extraversion may be suitable to be representatives, public relation officers, teachers etc. As per the above statement extroverts show relationship towards achievement.

Eysenck believed that purely extrovert or purely introvert people were rarely found and he therefore preferred to use a dimension i.e. a continuum ranging from introversion to extroversion instead or-naming types as introverts and extroverts. Generally Neuroticism will have negative effect in teaching.

1.2.3 Characteristics of Personality:

The results of various experimental studies and observations have led to the identification of the following characteristics of personality.

1) Personality is something unique and specific.
2) Personality exhibits self-consciousness.
3) Personality includes all the behavior patterns.
4) Personality is not just a collection of so many traits or characteristics.
5) Personality cannot be said to be static, it is dynamic and

continuously in the process of change and modification.

6) Every personality is the product of heredity and environment.
7) Learning and acquisition of experiences contribute towards growth and development of personality. Every personality is the end product of this process of learning and acquisition.
8) Personality of an individual can be described as well as measured.
9) Personality should not be taken as synonymous with one's character. Personality is a psychological concept is more comprehensive term, which includes character as one of its constituents.
10) Personality should also be viewed differently from the ego or individual self.
11) Every person's personality has one more distinguishing feature that is aiming to an end or towards some specific goals.

Practical definition of personality may be said that "personality is a complex blend of constantly evolving and changing patterns of one's unique behavior emerged as a result of one's interaction with one's environment and directed towards some specific ends.

1.2.4 Components of Personality:

While there are many different theories of personality, the first step is to understand exactly what is meant by the term *personality.* A brief definition would be that personality is made up the characteristic patterns of thoughts, feelings, and behaviors that make a person unique. In addition to this, personality arises from within the individual and remains fairly consistent throughout life.

Consistency - There is generally a recognizable order and regularity to behaviors. Essentially, people act in the same ways or similar ways in a variety of situations.

Psychological and physiological - Personality is a psychological construct, but research suggests that it is also influenced by biological processes and needs.

Impact behaviors and actions - Personality does not just influence how we move and respond in our environment; it also causes us to act in certain ways.

Multiple expressions - Personality is displayed in more than just behavior. It can also be seen in our thoughts, feelings, close relationships, and other social interactions.

1.2.5 Theories of Personality:

There are a number of different theories about how personality develops. Different schools of thought in psychology influence many of these theories. Some of these major perspectives on personality include:

a. Type Theories:

Type theories are the early perspectives on personality. These theories suggested that there are a limited number of "personality types" which are related to biological influences.

b. Trait Theories:

Gordon Allport is to the trait tradition. He regarded language as the source of information about human nature. Allport also proposed that personality was idiographic, meaning that each person is unique and that some traits may only be possessed by one person – making comparisons across individuals impossible. The nomothetic approach takes the opposite belief in that it emphasizes comparisons among people and that a trait is defined in the same manner across the population. Allport did not entirely disregard the nomothetic approach; however, he believed that "even the traits that people seem to share with one another always have a personal flavor that differs from individual to individual (Carver & Scheier).

Raymond Cattell has been a very important contributor to this framework and argued very strongly that empirical study was essential when trying to determine which traits underlie human behavior (Carver & Scheier). He presumed that the "importance of a trait is reflected in how many words describe it" (Carver & Scheier). The presumption is also called the lexicon criterion. After much data collection and analysis, Cattell deduced that personality could be captured in a set of sixteen dimensions, five factor model "the big five".

The first evidence of the big five model was published in 1949, when D. W. Fiske attempted to reproduce Cattell's 16-factor structure, but failed. Instead he founded a five-factor solution. However, not until the 1980's did this model become more widely accepted. There has been some disagreement about the precise labeling of each factor, but the most commonly used are the following: extraversion, agreeableness, conscientiousness, neuroticism, and openness to experience (McCrae & John). The claim of these theorists is that these five factors, singly or in combination, can be found in virtually all personality constructs.

The first factor, extraversion, is best characterized by assertiveness or an open expression of impulses. The second factor is agreeableness. Agreeableness is essentially not only being "warm and likeable" but it also encompasses a sense of nurturing and emotional supportiveness (Carver & Scheier). The third factor, conscientiousness, is a bit more abstract. It most often reflects qualities such as "planning, persistence, and purposeful striving toward goals" (Carver & Scheier). It can also be thought of as simply one's will. Neuroticism, or emotionality, encompasses emotional control as well as emotional anxiety. . Openness to experience is the fifth and final factor. Although there is much debate as to what this factor ultimately entails, it mostly resembles both the imaginative side of intellect as well as the logical side (Carver & Scheier, McCrae & Oliver). Trait theories viewed personality as the result of internal characteristics that are genetically based.

c. Psychodynamic Theories:

The psychoanalytical approach of Freud personality is made up of three interdependent psychological forces: the id, the ego, and the superego. According to Freud, behavior is a function of the interaction of these three systems (Hogan).

d. Behavioral Theories:

Behavioral theories suggest that personality is a result of interaction between the individual and the environment. Behavioral theorists study observable and measurable behaviors, rejecting theories that take internal thoughts and feelings into account. Behavioral theorists include B. F. Skinner and John Watson.

e. Humanist Theories:

Emphasize the importance of free will and individual experience in the development of personality. Humanist theorists include Carl Rogers and Abraham Maslow.

1.2.6 Personality Assessment:

We can only make an estimate or assessment of personality, as the true measurement of one's personality is not possible. This assessment can be made by means of a variety of techniques like observation, rating scale, interview & situation test, questionnaire personality inventory & projective technique.

Correlational method (i) permits study of a broad range of individual difference variables. (ii) Permits study of variables in natural, real world setting (iii) may determine whether information on one variable can be used to predict a second variable in the future.

In projective technique all kind of perceptual and creative

activities have been utilized. It attempts to probe unconscious aspects of personality by having people project their feeling needs and values in to the interpretation of ambiguous stimuli. It is used to assess the total personality of the individual rather than in fragments. Ink blot Test, TAT, CAT are used on subjects of different cultural, educational, medical and social group.

1.2.7 The Importance of Teacher Personality:

Teacher "The teacher is the actual builder of the nation"

What counts above all is the impact of the personality of teacher on the young and growing minds. It is the character, integrity and personality of the teacher that counts thousand times more than imparting mere bookish and theoretical knowledge. It is also generally believed that "the inspiration exaltation, confidence and the strength that the student receives from his teacher takes him gradually to the glorious height of achievement, making him thoroughly, equipped to lead a balanced and ideal life". Thus, the importance of teachers' personality and character are linked with future of the children.

What is even more significant, people from a cross section of occupational groups and regions recognize the teachers as the most critical agents in the learning process and their role as the most potent instrument for the successful implementation of educational policies and programmes. These issues include the role and importance of teachers in the educational process, Quality of teachers and importance of teacher's personality.

Personality may be viewed as the dynamic organization of those traits and characteristic patterns of behavior that are unique to the individual (Callahan, 1966). Some social psychologists take the position that personality is purely a matter of social perception - which it is meaningless to speak of anyone's personality apart from the particular people who interact with him, get impressions about him, and use trait terms in describing him (Holt, 1971). A trait is a simple behavioral pattern - a disposition or tendency to behave in a describable way.

According to Allport (1966), a trait

1) Is more generalized than a habit.
2) Is dynamic and determinative in behavior?
3) May be viewed either in the light of the personality which contains it, or in the light of its distribution in the population at large.
4) Cannot be proved nonexistent by the sheer fact that some acts are inconsistent with it.

Research on teacher personality is based on the assumption that the teacher as a person is a significant variable in the teaching-learning process. Personality influences the behavior of the teacher in diverse ways, such as interaction with students, methods selected, and learning experiences chosen (Murray, 1972).

The effective use of a teacher's personality is essential in conducting instructional activities. Personality aids teaching, for communication takes place between the teacher and the learner, even in the absence of the spoken word (nonverbal communication). The teacher whose personality helps create and maintain a classroom or learning environment in which students feel comfortable and in which they are motivated to learn is said to have a desirable teaching personality (Callahan, 1966). Each individual has characteristic attributes of personality which influence both the manner in which he behaves toward others and the ways in which they respond to him. The teacher with pervasive authoritarian characteristics, for example, is likely to reflect them in his relationships with students and in the techniques he uses in his instruction (Morrison and Mclntyre, 1972.)

The school is more than a place where knowledge and skills are taught and learned: it is a miniature community in itself where members interact and influence the behavior of each other (Shoben,

1962). The nature of interactions and influences in the school is an important factor in determining the learner's perceptions of school and his attitudes toward school-related persons and activities (Finley, 1969). This factor involves the interplay between the personality of the teacher and that of the learner. According to Khan and Weiss (1973), it can be postulated from the theory of interpersonal perception that a learner's attitudes toward the teacher will affect his attitudes toward the courses taught by the teacher and toward the school. It may be further postulated that the learner's attitude toward a teacher is a function of the teacher's personality. Nelson (1964) reported that teachers and pupils in junior high school deviate significantly in terms of their attitudes toward each other. He found that teachers are cognitively oriented toward pupils while pupils are affectively oriented toward teachers.

Teacher personality is, therefore, directly and indirectly related to learning and teaching in the affective domain as well as to that in cognitive and psychomotor domains. Reports of great teachers commonly stress their personalities, rather than their scholarship or technical teaching skills. If we are to be concerned with the student's development of identity, Hilgard (1965) suggests that we should not be afraid of showing feeling. Objectivity can be served by showing that there are those who believe otherwise, but we need not do obeisance to other viewpoints by sterilizing our own enthusiasm into a vapid eclecticism. Erikson (1964) distinguishes between the identifications that help shape a growing personality, and the identity that is later achieved. That is, the child identifies himself with significant people, such as parents and teachers, and incorporates attitudes, ideals, and personality traits from them.

1.3 Teaching Competency:

Teaching constitutes one of the major tasks of a teacher. Competency over this task of teaching is the essence of a successful educational system. The development of teaching competence among teachers necessitates a clear understanding of the term as well as the method for its assessment. The term teaching is defined in different ways. The analytical approach to perceive teaching has given a basis for innovations in teacher educations, like microteaching. The term 'competency' has also been a debatable term. It refers to the criteria that determine teacher effectiveness. The term 'teaching competency' as defined by various authors, it included knowledge, attitudes, and skills and other teacher characteristics. Some others perceive teacher competence as teacher's behaviors that produce intended efforts.

Teaching is skilled job and complex task. It is done for the pupils. That is to bring desirable changes or improvement in their behaviors. Success of this operation depends up on a good planning and mastery execution. The educationist, psychologist, research workers and the teachers working in the field have establish some general principles and maxims of teaching, which may prove quite helpful in making the task of teaching quite effective and purposeful.

1.2.4 What Is a Competency?

Before defining the various competencies of a quality instructor, an explanation of what is meant by a competency in the first place should be addressed. One could come up with any number of definitions of the term competency. Various lexical definitions (American Heritage Publishing Company, 2000; Merriam-Webster, 1997; Miller, 2006; MSN, 2006) were considered along with implied definitions Once all of the sources had been compiled and carefully considered, a definition that expressed the intent of competency in an online education setting was generated, herein competency will refer to appropriate prior knowledge, skills, attitudes, and abilities in a given context that adjust and develop with time and needs in order to effectively and efficiently accomplish a task and that are measured against a minimum standard.

But what does it mean to be competent? It is more than simply an alignment to a competency. It is only a guide laying out the knowledge, skills, attitudes, and abilities expected in a competent instructor. To be competent is not the awareness, the attainment, or even the knowledge of the various attributes within the document, although all of these play a part. To be competent is the juxtaposition of this knowledge with the application of that knowledge in a teaching practice. In other words, a competent individual is one who effectively and efficiently accomplishes a task [instructs] in a given context, using appropriate knowledge, skills, attitudes, and abilities that have adjusted and developed with time and needs.

1.2.4 Meaning of Teaching Competency:

Modern thoughts and scientific technological advancements have given an orientation to teacher competence. According to Karl Masanari, "competence based education or performance based teacher education has the potential to revolutionalize the entire field of educational personal development through its emphasis on clearly stated role derived objectives, the individualization and personalization instruction". In the words of Murthy and Lulla, "competency based teacher education is that type of professional education of classroom teachers that takes the predetermined competence of behaviors as the base of teacher education programmer".

1.2.4 Major Dimensions of a Competency Based Teaching Five Performance Areas

1. Performance in the Classroom:

Including teaching and learning processes, evaluation techniques and classroom management.

2. School-level performance:

Including organization of morning assembly elaboration of national social and cultural events; and participation in school level management.

3. Performance in Out-of School Activities:

Including such educational activities as field visits of learners, observation tours, etc.

4. Performance Related to Parental Contact and Co-Operation:

Including such matters, as enrolment and retention, regularity in attendance, discussion progress reports, improving quality of achievement,etc.

5. Performance Related to Community Contact and Co-Operation:

Including such issues as VEC work, joint celebration of certain events by the community support in the development of the school, etc. In order to equip teachers well in these performance areas and to enable them to become thoroughly competent to carry out these professional tasks with efficiency and insight, ten competency areas have been identified. The competency areas are designed to provide adequate theoretical and conceptual understanding and to empower teachers to perform their responsibilities with professional insight and confidence. In essence, these are teacher competencies which should eventually aim at the development of learner competencies and qualities at the school stage. To achieve these multiple goals, teacher competences include relevant conceptual elements, content Siemens, contextual aspects, transactional and evaluation aspects, etc. The entire ten competency areas thus identified converges on one or more of performance areas and interrelate theory and practice in a focused manner. Specific competencies under each area indicated as example in the NCTL publications on this subject.

While professional competencies such as those enumerated above are necessary for every teacher to master, it has been observed that they by themselves do not alter result in effective performance. This has been a problem of many school systems not only in India but also in many other Countries of the world. Teacher effectiveness is not automatically ensured by professional competencies and practical skills only. One of the reasons of the phenomenon is that the actual performance of trained teachers in the classroom or schools in a consistent manner equally dependent, if not more, on their commitment to perform well. It is this commitment component that plays a decisive role in effective teacher education. Thus, well trained and effective teachers are those both competent and committed professional practitioners.

1.2.5 Effective Teaching:

As such teaching is a complex set of attitudes, knowledge, skills, motivation and values. Effective teaching varies from mere teaching. Additional learning mentioned in the above areas might lead to effective teaching and learning. The improvement of learning requires an awareness of the complex relationship among faculty, students and institutions. There is no single method for effective teaching and learning.

Effective teaching leads to engaged and intelligent learning. It may be defined as showing are helping students to learn how to do something, giving instructions, guiding in the study of something, providing with knowledge, besides causing to know and understand. It is also guiding and facilitating learning, enabling the learner to learn, setting the condition for learning.

Effective teaching is much more than an intuitive process. Holistic appreciation, active knowledge, teamwork, critical thinking, creative thinking, and problem solving are the major outcomes of effective teaching.

Definition:

'Teaching effectiveness is the ability and interaction between the physical, intellectual and psychological interest of the students, content matter, ability of the teachers and the evaluative procedures' (Good. 1959).

Flanders and Simon (1969) defined Teaching effectiveness as, "a sense of humor, ability to explain, ability to understand, ability to manage class and helping and being fair with the students".

Rajagopalan (1976) defined Teaching effectiveness as, "an ability to produce good results. Thus teaching effectiveness is the activity and out interaction between the physical, intellectual and psychological increase of the student and some given subject content, the ability of the teacher to relate the learning activities to the developmental process of the learner and to their current and future interests and needs".

An effective teacher possesses the better personality adjustment and favorable attitudes (Ahhaya, 1974). Presenting the lesson in an interesting manner attains top most priority in the components of effective teaching (Srinivasan, 1991).

Saying about Effective Teachers:

'An ordinary teacher tells

A good teacher demonstrates

The best teacher inspires'.

Thus in an effective teaching process a teacher is,

- an inspirer
- a frame worker
- a facilitator

- an impartial guide
- an creator of knowledge
- a classroom manager
- an self-evaluator
- an organizer

Research suggests that the following characteristics are important for an effective teaching.

The effective teacher will

- Provide a safe psychological climate for all pupils.
- Not be too dominant.
- Know each pupil individually by name.
- Show knowledge of the pupil's background.
- Ask thought-provoking questions.
- Be aware of social groupings within the class.
- Be a good organizer and a leader.
- Encourage warm relationships among pupils.

Generally teaching employs a variety of methods and techniques. Among these teachers, only a few, make learning effective, that is to enable the students to acquire knowledge, and develop understanding, ability to apply, necessary skills, ability to appreciate, etc. In the words of William Arthur Ward, "the mediocre teacher tells, the good teacher explains the superior teacher demonstrates the great teacher inspires". The great teacher inspires students by influencing them by this teaching and by his qualities. The teacher has to satisfy the intellectual curiosity of the learner and make further challenges on his intellectual ability by presenting the subject matter. No doubt it requires hard work, involvement and devotion to his work. So it is not only the string of degrees that makes a good teacher but the qualities such as alertness, integrity, sensitivity, enthusiasm and positive attitude to work and life. If the nation is blessed with right type of teachers equipped with necessary knowledge and skills to influence their students to learn well, to have right values, and to inculcate right attitude, progress would be immense in all spheres of life. Thus, the effective teacher is a supreme factor in any educational system.

1.2.4 Factors for Effective Teaching:

The first and foremost factor that contributes to the effective teaching is the attitude of the teachers towards their profession. An effective teacher must have a devotional attitude towards teaching. He must love his job and should be prepared to subordinate his personal interest to the interest of his pupils and to that of his institution. He should possess a spirit of selfless service.

This type of attitude no doubt is essential for success in any profession. But it is more essential in the case of teaching.

The duty of a teacher is of vital importance in the development of the human resources of a country. The success of any educational system depends upon the teachers.

The Secondary Educational Commission (1953) has rightly observed that the most important factor in the contemplated educational system is the teacher and the place he occupies in the school as well as in the community. Productivity on a job is determined largely by the way the worker feels about the job or his attitude towards it. Any amount of money spent on education will be futile if we are not able to draw out the best from it. It is unthinkable to have education with at values. All the educational commissions have stressed inculcation of moral, religious, aesthetic, economic, political and social values through value education.

The fundamental aim of education is to shape an integrated personality though physical, intellectual, emotional and ethical values. While great changes have occurred in the human evolution, the external values continue to be the essential constituents of progress and peace of the human race. It is education that has to build the essential human values in human beings. Parents place their complete trust in teaches regarding the welfare of their children. The society also expects much from the educational institutions, which form the ethos of all human development. The role of teachers and educational institutions in inculcating value education is highlighted in the recommendations of important educationists and learned bodies in India and abroad. Without values life becomes a series of meaningless events. So it is essential to transform the system of education qualitatively in terms of value, content, standards of relevance to life etc. the role of education is to promote humanistic outlook, sense of brotherhood and a commitment to promotion of ethical and cultural values.

1.2.4 Meaning of Teaching Effectiveness:

Teaching effectiveness related to the successful functioning of teacher. It implies the extent to which a teacher can teach successfully in the class. The real function of a teacher is to be able to teach effectively and successfully in the class. This in turn depends upon a number of factors that may be studied and analyzed for the general guidance of teachers and would-be-teachers. This is been found that all the teachers cannot teach equally successfully. The efficiency and effectiveness of teachers defer widely. This means that there are certain factors that are responsible for effective and not-so-effective teaching in the class. These factors must be analyzed as far as possible, so that teacher effectiveness may be determined on their bases. Previously, the general belief was that anybody who possesses a certain type of knowledge could teach the same to the pupils. In other words, a good scholar was also considered being a good teacher. But, now it has been found that this idea is not correct. A good scholar may be a good or a bad teacher. This means that teaching involves certain other factors, which are responsible for its effectiveness. The objective of this study therefore, is to ascertain those factors that are responsible for the success and effectiveness.

1.2.4 Determinates of Teaching Effectiveness:

More commonly effectiveness is seen in terms of personal achievement characteristics, such as:

- Pupil's performance in examination
- Classroom control
- Completing the course in the time allocated
- Being a warm, encouraging, courteous person with a sense of humor
- The frequency of using good teaching strategies.

1.2.4 Teaching Effectiveness Assessed by the Three Types of Criteria:

a) Process as a criterion:

By process we mean performance and behavior of the teacher as well as performance and behavior of students and the student teacher interaction in the classroom. According to this criterion, the best test of teaching-effectiveness is what the teacher does in the classroom, what the students do, and the interaction that takes place between the teacher and the students. Accordingly, teaching effectiveness is assessed through observation of teacher behavior and student behavior, and their mutual interaction.

b) Product as a Criterion:

By product we mean what is learned or the outcome of learning. Thus teaching effectiveness is ascertained by the achievement of the pupils. The objective of teaching is to make students learn. Therefore, learning on the part of the students is the real test of good teaching. The proof of the pudding lies in its eating. Therefore, the product or the actual learning by the students is the real criterion for assessing teaching effectiveness.

c) **Presage as a Criterion:**

Presage refers to the academic achievements and personal characteristics of teachers. According to this view, the best test of teacher effectiveness is the intellectual attainments of the teacher, the education and training received by him, his personal qualities and characteristics.

1.2.5 Teaching Competencies - General and Specific:

David G. Rayns (1969) "In characteristic of characteristic of teacher" described the two types of teacher competencies. "Teaching is complex and many sided task demanding a variety of human traits and abilities. These may be roughed into two major categories. For those involving the teachers mental abilities and skills, his understandings of psychological and education principles and his knowledge of general & specific subject matter to be taught and second those qualities stemming from the teachers personality, his interest, attitudes and beliefs, his behaviors in working relationships with pupils and other individuals and the like".

A to Z of Teaching Competencies:

'A' is for alertness

'B' is for to keep busy in worthwhile tasks

'C' is for clarity

'D' is for devotion and discovery

'E' is for enthusiasm and evaluation

'F' is for feedback for the guidance of the learner and the Teacher himself

'G' is for goal setting and achieving

'H' is for hard work, honest work

'I' is for involvement of children

'J' is for judicious attitude and just action

'K' is for knowledge of student, subject matter and oneself

'L' is for linking learning with daily experiences and life

'M' is for motivation

'N' is for need –based learning

'O' is for objectivity

'P' is for practice and praising children when needed

'Q' is for quiz organizing for monitoring learning process

'R' is for relationship and review

'S' is for stimulation

'T' is for tolerance and technology of teaching learning

'U' is for unbiased attitude

'V' is for variety of learning experience.

'W' is for warmth and wisdom.

'X' is for x-ray of learning process

'Y' is for yearning and eagerness

'Z' is for zeal

Definition:

The term teaching competency is defined by various authors includes more than mere teacher effects or pupil. According to some authors it includes knowledge, attitude, skill and other teacher characteristics (Haskew 1956, Wilson 1973). Some others perceive teacher competence as teacher behaviors that produce intended effects (Medley and Mitzel-1973, Beiddle-1964).

Arriving at a more comprehensive definition Rama- (1979) defines teacher competency as the ability of a teacher manifested through a set of over teacher classroom behaviors which is a resultant of the interaction between the presage and the product and the product variables of teaching with in a social setting". Thus the term "teaching" can be defined as a set of observable teacher behavior that facilitate or bring about pupil learning, and "teaching competency" means an effective performance of all the observable teachers behavior that bring about desired pupil outcomes. The term "competency" has also been a debatable term. It refers to the criteria that determine teacher effectiveness.

1.3.10 Components of Teaching Competency:

There are four components of teaching competencies: Knowledge, Performance, Behavior and Consequence. Consequence competency refers to the pupil's outcome or achievement. The other three competencies refer to the activities of the teacher in and outside the classroom.

- **Knowledge Competency** includes the content of the subject matter and the knowledge of the teacher over the subjects.
- **Performance Competency** refers to the report and the personality of the teacher.
- **Behavior Competency** refers to the rapport and the personality of the teacher.

Pictorial representation of the Components of teaching competency

Pictorial representation of the Components of teaching competency

Knowledge
Knowledge
Content
Organization
Teaching Competency
Performance
Clarity
Communication
Audio
Consequence
Behaviour

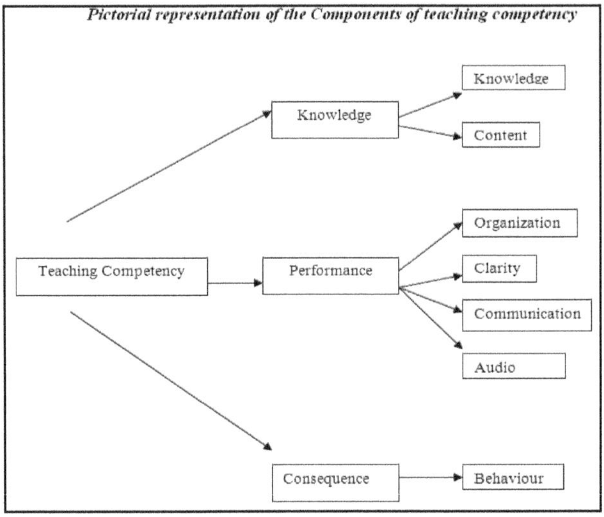

1.3.11 Competency – based teacher training strategy:

The basic teaching competencies are Cognitive based competencies, Performance based competencies, Affective based competencies, Consequence based competencies and Managerial competencies. These basic teaching Competencies having varying number of sub competencies as shown in the table below:

Competency – based teacher training strategy

▲

Basic teaching competencies taken	Cognitive based Competencies	Performance based Competencies	Affective based Competencies	Consequence based Competencies	Managerial Competencies
Sub-Competencies taken	(i) Writing instructional objectives (ii)Assigning home work (iii) Developing problem solving ability	(i) Writing on black board (ii) Explaining (iii)Lustrating with examples (iv) Gaining and sustaining attention (v)Fluency in questioning (vi) Probing questioning	(i) Increasing performance pupil participation (ii) Recognizing attending behavior of students (iii) Developing social values in students	(i) Giving reinforcement (ii) Evaluating student Learning	(i) Managing supportive classroom environment (ii) Maintaining classroom discipline (iii) Using teaching aids

Competencies based teacher education program identify the objectives, the criteria, the performance indicators and criterion levels so clearly for the student that she/he can assess himself/herself whether or not the objective has been met. This teacher-training program and educational policy development need to include the requisite teacher competencies. This will provide policy functional and practical help for successful teaching.

1.4 Personality and Teaching Competency:

The relationship between personality and teaching competency play an important role. At all levels of education personal factors have been found to exert influence on teaching. In teaching profession one needs to have good teaching competency and personality, enhances teaching competencies. Mallik (1984) found personality factors like intelligence, emotional stability, tender mindedness self sufficiency, placidity and relaxedness environmental factors like physical environment, democracy, goal direction, satisfaction, formality, age and experience were associated with teaching success in science.

Research on brain based learning suggests the personality factor is fundamental to effective teaching. A teacher who is skilled in terms of personality will naturally try to build a serve of mutual understanding, group feeling and a climate of trust by encouraging students to communicate freely. According to a report of the national center for clinical infant programs, the most critical elements for a teacher's success in school is an understanding of how to teach or his teaching competency (Gole man 1998).The key ingredients for his understanding are confidence, curiosity, commitment, self control, relatedness, capacity to communicate ability to co-operate etc. Traits are all aspects of personality. Hence, the present study believes that there is a correlation between personality and teaching competency.

1.5 Need for the Study:

Teachers Personality and teaching competencies play an important role in teaching profession. In the midst of hectic life prevailing in the modern world, a teacher should have good personality and his/her teaching should be competent-based. If the teachers are competent and have balanced personality, the entire nation will be benefited.

The present centaury throws a number of challenges before the teachers. For working satisfactorily, the teachers should know how to adjust, how to manage the class, how to teach the students and how to contribute with full potential towards institutional goals as well as towards the welfare of the society and the nation at large. This is possible when the personality of the teacher trainee is properly molded. Unfortunately, our educational set up emphasis only on the cognitive aspect of the human resources, whereas the personality aspect of human resources is neglected. Personality factors are important, sometimes more than the academic competence. However good may be the system of education, curriculum and text books, if the teachers are not competent, education by and large will be ineffective. Therefore, the personality factors and teaching competency of the B.Ed. student's teachers play a vital role in their successful survival and fitness in the profession. Hence there is need for the present study.

1.6 Statement of the Problem:

"A study on Personality and Teaching Competency of B.Ed. Student teachers."

1.7 Significance of the Problem:

Healthy development of the individual and his personality may be regarded as one of the aims of education. Education has to be arranged that it helps the process of personality development. It is well know that teaching is influenced by personality characteristics of teacher. In the words of secondary education commission (1952-53), every teacher and educationalist of experiences knows that even the best curriculum and the perfect syllabus remains dead, unless quickened in to life by right methods of teaching and right kind of teachers. However good may be the system of education, curriculum and textbooks if the teachers are not efficient, competent and if the teachers are not well balanced in their personality then education by and large will be ineffective.

Teachers play an important role in the academic achievement of pupils. It is the responsibility of the teacher to make the pupils to grow in the full status in the overall development. Teacher should provide the necessary experiences and training to the pupil and ensure them to behave as per the expectations of society and lead a successful life. In order to succeed in such duties the teacher should be more efficient and alert.

The student teachers are at the threshold of entering into the career of teaching. Personality plays an important role in teaching profession. A student teacher should have good personality charters in the midst of hectic life prevailing in the modern world. The future of a nation depends upon the role played by the members of the teaching community. It is a pleasant privilege of the teacher, to shape the children of the nation into useful citizens of tomorrow. Therefore personality and teaching competency of the student teacher should be developed to face the growing, which in turn enhance their teaching performance.

Corey (1964) comments on the practicability of research as "No educational research project shall be undertaken unless its consequences give promise of improving significantly an important educational practice or operation".

By considering this is mind the present study was undertaken by the researcher to identify the level of personality characteristics and teaching competency of the student teachers. In the present study an attempt was made to find out the inner relationship among personality and teaching competency of B.Ed., student teachers. Definitely this study will lead to better understanding of the proper conditions for the maintenance of the good personality and teaching competency of the student teachers.

1.8 Operational Definitions:

(i) Personality:

Eysenck (1960) defined personality as more or loss stable and enduring organization of a person's character and temperament, intellect and physique which determine his unique adjustment to the environment.

According to Eysenck (1968) extra version refers to impulsive behavior with sociable tendencies. High scores on extraversion are indication of outgoing, impulsive and uninhibited behavior.

According to Eysenck neuroticism refers to an emotional, over responsiveness, emotional liability to neurotic breakdown under stress. High scoring individuals tend to be anxious, worrying and depressed. The neurotic has a tending to worry over little things to be unable to sleep make his mind. He feels inadequate to sleep in the night due to tenseness. He has illogical fear and is purred by troublesome thoughts a neurotic is a needed medical care and treat unit.

It refers to the score secured by the individual in H.J. Eysenck's M.P.I. The score secured by the individual in H.J. Eysenck's inventory is considered as the index of his/her personality

(ii) Teaching Competency:

It refers to the score secured by the individual in the Teaching Competency constructed by B.K Passi and M.S. Lalitha and the investigator. The actual score is 147; the investigator has converted it to

100. Therefore the score secured by the individual in the Teaching Competency is considered as the index of his/her Teaching Competency.

(iii) B.Ed. Student Teachers:

B.Ed. Student Teachers are those students who undergo one year theoretical and practical teacher training program after their graduation as a preparation for their teaching profession. They are also known as Student Teachers.

(iv) Sex:

Sex has its own type of function and norms. Therefore, the mean scores of both male and female student teachers are included in the present study to find out significant difference between them in their personality and teaching competencies.__In the present sample there are 84 male student teachers and 219 female student teachers.

(v) School Medium of Instruction:

The Medium of Instruction in which the student teachers had studied at the school level may exert influences on the present study. In this study teachers are divided into two groups – English medium and Tamil medium. In the present_sample there are 64 English medium student teachers and 238 Tamil medium student teachers.

(vi) Type of admission:

The type of admission in which the student teacher admitted may have a significant influence on present study, one group admitted to the various B.Ed. colleges through entrance exam (CENTAC- Central Admission Committee) conducted by Government and another group admitted to the various B.Ed. colleges through entrance exam (CET- Common Entrance Test) conducted by private B.Ed. colleges In the present sample there are 72 student teachers who were admitted by CENTAC and 231 student teachers who were admitted by CET.

(vii) Type of College:

The type of college in which the student teacher studied may have a significant influence on present study; the colleges are divided into two groups managed by Government and managed by private. In the present sample there are_170 student teachers who were studied in Private colleges and 133 student teachers who were studied in Government colleges.

(viii) Subject Specialization:

The subject specification may also exert influence on the present study. So the student teachers are divided into two groups namely Science and Arts. In the present sample there are_123 student teachers who belong to science group and 120 student teachers who belong to arts group.

(ix) Educational Qualification:

Educational qualification may also exert influence on the personality and teaching competencies of the student teacher. In this study, student teachers are divided into two groups namely Undergraduates and Postgraduates. In the present sample there are 230 student teachers who were graduates and 73 student teachers were post-graduates

(x) Teaching Experience:

Teaching experience of the student teachers may exert influence on the present study. They are divided into two groups namely experienced and inexperienced student teachers. In the present sample there are 31 student teachers who have teaching experience and 272 student teachers who do not have teaching experience.

(xi) Locality of Residence:

Residence of student teachers of both rural and urban are included in the study to find out whether there is any significant difference between the rural and urban student teachers regarding their personality and teaching competence. In the present sample there are 193 student teachers who belong to urban area and 110 student teachers who belong to rural.

(xii) Parents Educational Qualification:

Parent's educational qualification may also exert influence on the personality and teaching competencies of the student teacher. In this study, the parents are divided into four groups namely Undergraduates, Postgraduates, who have completed Higher Secondary (HSS) and those who are below SSLC. However in our study Parents Educational Qualification refers only to Father's Educational Qualification.

1.9 Objectives of the Study:

Primary Objectives:

- To study the personality characteristics of B.Ed. student teachers.
- To study the level of teaching competency of B.Ed. student teachers.
- To study the relationship, if any, between the Neuroticism and teaching competency of B.Ed. student teachers.
- To study the relationship, if any, between the extraversion and teaching competency of B.Ed. student teachers.
- To study the relationship, if any, between the Neuroticism and Extraversion of B.Ed. student teachers

Secondary Objectives:

1) To find out the difference, if any, between the groups in their personality characteristics of B.Ed. Student Teachers regarding the following background variables:

i) Sex
ii) Medium of the schools
iii) Type of admission
iv) Type of college studied
v) Subject specification
vi) Educational qualification
vii) Teaching experience
viii) Locality of residence
ix) Parents educational qualification

2) To find out the difference, if any, between the groups in their Teaching Competency of B.Ed. Student Teachers regarding the following background variables.

i) Sex
ii) Medium of the schools
iii) Type of school studied
iv) Type of college studied
v) Subject specification
vi) Educational qualification
vii) Teaching experience
viii) Locality of residence
ix) Parents educational qualification

1.10 Hypotheses of the Study:

The hypotheses of the study formed in the light of objectives and review of related literature are as follows:

1. The level of teaching competency of B.Ed. student teacher is high.

2. There is no significant relationship between extraversion and teaching competency of the B.Ed. student teachers.
3. There is no significant relationship between Neuroticism and teaching competency of the B.Ed. student teachers.
4. There is no significant difference between the mean scores of Neuroticism scores of male and female B.Ed. student teachers.
5. There is no significant difference between the mean scores of Extraversion scores of male and female B.Ed. student teachers
6. There is no significant difference between the mean scores of the Neuroticism scores of B.Ed. student teachers who had studied in Tamil medium and English medium at the school level.
7. There is no significant difference between the mean scores of the Extraversion scores of B.Ed. student teachers who had studied in Tamil medium and English medium at the school level.
8. There is no significant difference between the mean scores of the Neuroticism scores of B.Ed. student teachers who had admitted through CENTAC and CET.
9. There is no significant difference between the mean scores of the Extraversion scores of B.Ed. student teachers who had admitted through CENTAC and CET.
10. There is no significant difference between the mean scores of the Neuroticism scores of B.Ed. student teachers who had studied in private colleges and government colleges.
11. There is no significant difference between the mean scores of the Extraversion scores of B.Ed. student teachers who had studied in private colleges and government colleges.

12. There is no significant difference in the mean scores of Neuroticism scores of Science and Arts group of B.Ed. student teachers.
13. There is no significant difference in the mean scores of Extraversion scores of Science and Arts group of B.Ed. student teachers.
14. There is no significant difference between the mean scores of the Neuroticism scores in the Educational qualification of B.Ed. student teachers.
15. There is no significant difference between the mean scores of the Extraversion scores in the Educational qualification of B.Ed. student teachers.
16. There is no significant difference between the mean scores of the Neuroticism scores of B.Ed. student teachers who have teaching experience and those who do not have teaching experience.
17. There is no significant difference between the mean scores of the Extraversion scores of B.Ed. student teachers who have teaching experience and those who do not have teaching experience.
18. There is no significant difference between the mean scores of the Neuroticism scores of B.Ed. student teachers who had studied in urban and rural students.
19. There is no significant difference between the mean scores of the Extraversion scores of B.Ed. student teachers who had studied in urban and rural students.
20. There is no significant difference between the mean scores of the Neuroticism scores of B.Ed. student teachers with regard to the variable parental educational qualification.

21. There is no significant difference between the mean scores of the Extraversion scores of B.Ed. student teachers with regard to the variable parental educational qualification.
22. There is no significant difference between the mean scores of the teaching competency scores of male and female B.Ed. student teachers.
23. There is no significant difference between the mean scores of the teaching competency scores of B.Ed. student teachers whose medium of instruction at school level were English and Tamil.
24. There is no significant difference between the mean scores of the teaching competency scores of B.Ed. student teachers who had admitted through CENTAC and CET.
25. There is no significant difference between the mean scores of the teaching competency scores of B.Ed. student teachers who had studied in private colleges and government colleges.
26. There is no significant difference in the mean scores of teaching competency scores of science and arts group of B.Ed. student teachers.
27. There is no significant difference between the mean scores of the teaching competency scores of B.Ed. student teachers regarding the variable Educational qualification.
28. There is no significant difference between the mean scores of the teaching competency scores of B.Ed. student teachers who have teaching experience and those who do not have teaching experience.
29. There is no significant difference between the mean scores of the teaching competency scores of B.Ed. student teachers who had studied in urban and rural students.

30. There is no significant difference between the mean scores of the teaching competency scores of B.Ed. student teachers with regard to the parent's educational qualification.

1.11 Limitations of the Study:

1. The first limitation is the restrictiveness of the sample. The present study is limited to the B.Ed. colleges in Pondicherry region only. Karikal, Mahe and Yanam regions are not included.
2. The study is limited to B.ED student teachers of private Colleges
3. The H.J. Eysenck's M.P.I. is a self-report instrument with good reliability and validity. However, due to nature of self-report instrument, the participants in this study may have inadvertently miss marked an answer.
4. Since the time available for the study was very short, a detailed study was not possible to conduct by considering other psychological variable.
5. The main objective of the investigation is to study the relationship between the personality characteristics (neuroticism and extraversion) and teaching competency of B.Ed. student teachers alone is considered.

1.12 Overview of the Succeeding Chapters:

- Chapter II contains review of related literature for the present investigation carried out both in India and abroad.
- Chapter III deals with the methodology of the investigation viz. selection of tools and their administration.
- Chapter IV deals with the analysis and interpretation of data.
- Chapter V deals with summary, major findings, discussions, suggestions for further research, educational implications and conclusions.

2 Chapter

REVIEW OF LITERATURE

2.0 Introduction:

The phrase "review of literature" consists of two words: Review and Literature. The term 'review' means to organize the specific area of research to evolve and edifice the knowledge to show that her study would be an addition to this field. In research methodology, the term "literature" refers to the knowledge of a particular area of investigation of any discipline, which includes theoretical, practical and its research studies.

Review of related literature has a vital role as far as every research work is concerned. It is the basis for any research carried out in the related area. The related literature gives guidance and develops insight into the problem. As far as a student or a researcher is concerned, a familiarity with literature in any problem area helps him to discover what is already known, what others have attempted to find out, what methods have been prolific or disappointing and what problems remains to be solved. By examining what is already done about the problem, the investigator becomes familiar with various trends and phases in research in his/her area. Review of related literature ensures the avoidance of the unnecessary duplication too. The investigator attempted to collect the literature under the following titles:

In the previous chapter the genesis of the problem, need for the study and objectives of the study were discussed. In this chapter some of the related studies have been discussed. Only those studies which are in relation to the personality, extraversion, neuroticism and teaching competency are discussed.

In the words of Borg (1965), "the literature in any field forms the fundamental foundation upon which all the future work will be built". Study of related literature implies locating, reading and evaluating reports of research. This gives the researcher an understanding of the previous work which has been done in the area of interest. Related literature helps to give the investigator a more comprehensive idea about the concepts and definitions and gives them a clear direction and undertaking of how the study is to be proceeded.

The study of related literature helps him/her to adopt suitable design for the study. By understanding the limitation of the study, it ensures perfection in the study to be made. With these aims in view, the investigator has reviewed some of the important studies. The investigator traced out different types of research works like dissertation, thesis, relevant books on education and psychology and websites of psychiatry, education and psychology.

This chapter brings out a brief report on the trends of the research carried out by students of psychology and education on the Personality and Teaching Competency during the last few years.

The review of related literature is classified into,

i) Studies related to personality done in India and abroad.
ii) Studies related to teaching competency done in India and abroad.
iii) Synthesis of Review of Related Literature.

Studies Related to Personality Done in India and Abroad:

2.1 Research Studies Related To Personality Conducted Abroad:

Beck (1967) investigated 2,108 sixth-grade pupils' perception of teacher merit. He concluded that the pupils perceived the effective teacher as a warm, friendly and supportive person who communicates clearly, motivates and disciplines pupils effectively, and is flexible in methodology.

David E. Hunt, Bruce R. Joyce (1967) in their study, Teacher Trainee Personality and Initial Teaching Style, reveals that (1) the personality factors were substantially related to the leadership preference. (2) Preference for a democratic type of Leadership was negatively related to neuroticism and positively related to extraversion. (3) Personality factors exerted a directives influence upon individual's choice of an authoritarian type of leadership.

Walker's study (1969) was designed to investigate selected aspects of teacher personality in differing American high school environments, suggested that teachers in high creative schools are more adaptive, flexible, outgoing, permissive, and nurturant - factors considered important in fostering creativity.

Coats (1970) did a factor analysis of 42,810 student responses as student perceptions of teachers. It was found that a factor labeled teacher 'charisma' accounted for 61.5% of the variance in test items. It was concluded that teacher charisma is probably a significant factor of teacher effectiveness.

Eble , Hildebrand and Wilson (1970) in their study found number of characteristics, some of which are related to teacher personality, have been consistently identified as comprising effective teaching at the college and university level by. The major factors were found to be Clarity of organization, interpretation and explanation; encouragement of class discussion and the presentation of diverse points of view; stimulation of students' interests, motivation and thinking; manifestation of attentiveness to an interest in students; manifestation of enthusiasm.

McKeachie, Lin, and Mann (1971), in a comprehensive project by all items that had previously been used for student ratings of instructors and instruction in American colleges and universities were factor analyzed in a series of studies. Six stable factors that emerged were skill, overload (difficulty), structure, feedback, group interaction and student-teacher rapport (warmth). One of the findings was that the students of teachers who were high in 'rapport' (warmth) performed better on measures of critical thinking than did the other students.

Murray and Dandes (1972) had conducted a study of positive characteristics of successful teachers discovered by previous research efforts seem to be in line with Maslow's conceptualization of the self-actualizing person, whom he sees as a fully functioning, psychologically healthy individual possessing such attributes as acceptance, spontaneity, autonomy, democratic nature, and creativeness. Maslow (1970) suggests that the self-actualizing person is indeed the most effective teacher.

Cortis (1973) in his analysis of data on 127 primary teachers and 95 secondary teachers in English schools, he discerned that, by comparison with primary teachers, the secondary teachers tend to be more sensitive yet more tolerant in personality terms, to hold more progressive educational attitudes and to express a higher degree of satisfaction with teaching.

Thompson (1975), investigated longitudinally nearly 2,400 first- and fourth-year British secondary school pupils' attitudes toward school and teachers, confirmed the findings of Wright's study (1962) that what pupils find lacking in teachers are those qualities which make them human. She found that teachers tend to be seen as less happy, kind, fair and warm than other adults while excelling in wisdom, success and hardness. Those attributes seem to coincide with those of the teachers in traditional society. It was also found that attitudes toward both school and teachers change as pupil's progress through the system. Older pupils do not rate teachers as less human as they did when they were younger, but do rate them as less wise and successful

Edstrom's study (1976) explored the relations between certain cognitive and attitudinal characteristics and the instructional behavior of American elementary school teachers. All subjects (41 second-grade teachers and 54 fifth-grade teachers) took a battery of tests measuring aptitude, knowledge, cognitive style, and attitude. One of her findings indicated that more flexible teachers are better able to respond differentially to pupils without having to resort to using various organizational strategies (aides, groups, etc.) to produce individualization.

Haslett (1976) employed semantic differential scales to measure 667 American high school students' and 219 American college students' concept of a good teacher. She also compared her findings with those of previous studies on college instructors (Clinton, 1930; Bousfield, 1940; and Perry, 1971).

William J.F. Lew (1977) in his analysis of teaching and the teacher's personality, the investigation of student description of their ideal teacher, concluded that if teachers learned how the students wanted them to behave they would become more like the student ideal. the research findings and theories presented in this paper will help improve teacher characteristics, especially teacher personality, with a view to promoting teaching effectiveness and upgrading the quality of teaching.

Kenneth A. Feldman (1986) reviewing the extant research correlating college teachers'' personality (and related attitudinal) characteristics with the teachers'' effectiveness in the classroom (measured by the overall evaluations of the teachers'' students), the wide variety of personality traits that have been studied were grouped into 14 clusters of traits. Considering those studies measuring the teacher's personality characteristics through the teacher's self-reporting, only 4 of 14 trait clusters showed statistically significant average correlations between the teacher's personality traits and students"

Tiwari (1986) studied some personality and motivational Dynamics of employed, underemployed and unemployed educated youths. A study of some personality and motivational dynamics of employed, underemployed and unemployed educated youth. The major objectives of the study were to examine whether or not unemployed, underemployed and employed groups would differ in terms of their personality factors (anxiety, neuroticism, and extraversion). Eysenck personality Inventory (Hindi version) and other related tools were used. A sample of 300 youth 100 unemployed, 100 underemployed and 100 employed was drawn by adopting and incidental cum purposive sampling technique. The major conclusion was Neuroticism and extraversion were not good predictors of personality dynamics of the groups.

Janet R Rommel (1992)**,** the relationship of teacher personality types to classroom effectiveness with at-risk students in special education residential schools findings of the study did not substantiate the validity of specific personality types as effective teachers; there was a high correlation between the characteristics of the effective teachers and the body of research on effective teaching. Study suggested that agricultural education pre-service students differ in learning styles, personality styles, and in their preferred way of teaching.

Chan and Caputic (1998) had conducted a study for the critical evaluation of emotional intelligence scale (MEIS) to Australian graduates. The aim of the study revealed that EI was not related to IQ but was elated to specific personality measures (empathy) and to other criterion measures (life satisfaction). EI was also related to people's ability to manage their moods but not their ability to prevent moods from biasing their judgment. IQ was surprisingly related to both these mood process. The result suggests that EI construct is distinctive and useful.

King, Deborgah Hines (1998) had conducted a study on measurement of differences in EI of pre-service educational leadership of students and practicing administrators as measured by Multifactor Emotional Intelligence Scale (MEIS). The purpose of the study was to explore possible relationships between emotional intelligence and educational leadership. The major findings of this study can be generalized as practicing administrators scored for perceiving emotions, assimilations emotions and total emotional intelligence using expert and target scoring.

Liu (1999), in his study, Pre-service Teachers' Personality Types and Computer Achievement Research findings have suggested that students' computer achievement is a function of four computer attitude variables – enjoyment, motivation, importance, and anxiety. The more positive attitudes students have toward using and teach computers, the higher their computer achievement scores are likely to be. While studying computer attitudes, researchers found that a person's attitudes are subject to change in different learning environment or with different learning experiences.

Pyrari (1999) had conducted a study to find out the influence of emotional intelligence on academic achievement. The study realer that the emotional intelligence of boys was slightly greater than girls. No significant gender difference was observed in emotional instability, emotional regression and personality disintegration.

Bobbie Chan (2002) A Study of the Relationship Between Tutor's Personality and Teaching Effectiveness: Does Culture Make A Difference? This study reveals that Renqing, Face, Harmony and

Leadership significantly predict tutors' teaching effectiveness in the classroom environment. Certain facets from the distinctive indigenous factor of Chinese Tradition seem to be a useful complement to MBTI in predicting Chinese teaching attitudes and behavior. In particular, Harmony seems to be significantly related to all four dimensions of teaching.

Salovey P. (2002) had conducted a study on the relationship between emotional intelligence, personality and perceived quality of social relationship. They found that both EI and personality correlated with social relationship. Whether EI can predict individuals respond to traumatic stress. They found that individuals with higher EI scores, report lower psychological symptoms relating to their traumatic stress and traumatic stress had a greater impact on females than males and males had higher EI than females. They also found that individuals who use monitoring style would experience lower stress when compared to those who use blunting style. Monitors had higher EI scores than blunders.

Tracy Kitchel, Dr. Robert M. Torres, (2005) in their study, personality type as a predictor of interaction between student teachers and cooperating teachers. Findings suggest that, according to both cooperating teachers and student teachers, that student teachers were receiving psychosocial assistance from cooperating teachers. In addition, according to both student teachers and cooperating teachers, student teachers did not need much, nor did they receive much support related to roles and responsibilities of an agriculture teacher. Although the study found strength in relationships between overall perceived similarity and interaction satisfaction, personality type was found to have little influence on the variables.

Jan Vopalensky (2007)) in his study, the Influence of Teacher Personality on the Formation of Pupil Personality The problem of the individual's socialization as a permanent complex process, during which exogenic factors (social, political, cultural-ideological) become part of hierarchically arranged regulating systems of personality, is a relatively frequent subject of psychological research. Personalities, intellectual, emotional and social development in relationship to various socialization factors have been intensively studied.

2.2 Research Studies Related To Personality Conducted In India:

Rao (1963) investigated the role of certain aspects of personality and patterns of adjustment in scholastic performance. He concluded that the differences on achievement were found to be significantly related to aspects of personality like neurotic difficulties, academic achievement was found to be significantly related to the considered aspects of personality.

Stanley (1964) correlates personality with religious conversion. The reported results were obtained from questionnaire administrated to 347 Australian Theological students representing 8 Christian denominations. The administered subjects were the Extraversion and neuroticism scale of Maudsley personality inventory measures of conversion, fundamentalism etc. The following hypotheses were found to be significant as follows (i) There is negative correlation between neuroticism and conversion from one religion to another. (ii) There is a positive correlation between Extraversion and conversion form one religion to another.

Bhusan (1968) demonstrated a significant relationship between personality factors and preference for authoritarian or democratic leadership behaviour using standard personality inventory on 400 College undergraduates. Chi. square test, t- test were employed. Some of the major findings were (1) the personality factors were substantially related to the leadership preference. (2) Preference for a democratic type of Leadership was negatively related to neuroticism and positively related to extraversion. (3) Personality factors exerted a directives influence upon individual's choice of an authoritarian or democratic type of leadership etc. In a study with 150 randomly selected male arts students.

Sinha (1969) investigated the relation between introversion, extroversion and level of aspiration. Extroverts were found to set higher levels of aspiration in general. Under the condition of success both extroverts and introverts exhibited identical positive shifts in levels of aspiration. Extroverts showed move shifts in the marginal failure conditions, while introverts showed more shift in the miserable failure conditions.

Ansari (1974) studied flexibility-Rigidity, Personality trait among Indian Students. The objectives were (1) to study typical behaviours of rigid and non-rigid persons. (2) to find out the personality traits of rigid and non-rigid students and to study the relationship between rigidity and other personality characteristics. Rigidity scale of Rehfisch and Bernreater personality inventory (BPI) were used. Data were analyzed with the help of critical ratio and Correlational technique. Rigidity was not related to sex, parental occupational goals, type of education or regional differences. Rigidity was related to dominance, introversion and Neuroticism.

Jain (1974) examined" extreme response style as a personality factor. In a well designed study the author made it explicit that extreme response styles operated more consistently in females than in males. The data were collected with the help of Hindi version of Cattell's 16PF Questionnaire (1950) and other related tools. More than 500 boys and 500 girls were administered the picture reaction test. Out of these 50 boys and 50 girls who showed extreme responses were selected on the bases of Q I and Q3 on PRT scores. The age range was 17 years to 25 years.

Srivastara and Saxena (1979) made a comparative study on Personality correlates of self rated Academic success and Failure. A study was conducted to find out the personality characteristics of Indian students who rated themselves as academically successful and unsuccessful. The sample comprised 200 male students of whom 110 were successful in academic and 90 academically unsuccessful from the graduate classes in arts of two degrees colleges affiliated to Kanur University. Some of the findings were. Academically successful students were significantly lower on anxiety factor than successful students. Academically successful students were more extrovert than academically unsuccessful students.

Kumar (1980) correlates personality and Academic adjustment. The aim of the study was to ascertain the relationship between certain personality dimensions and academic adjustment of college students. Academic adjustment inventories (AAI), Eysenck Personality Inventory (EPI) were administered to a mixed sample of 500 undergraduate college students of Bihar University. Some of the major findings were no significant difference between the English and Hindi version of EPI was observed. The introvert student had better academic adjustment than extrovert students. The normal (or stables) Student had better academic adjustment than the neurotic (or unstable) students. The stable introvert students had the highest adjustment while unstable extrovert students had the lowest adjustment.

Sharma (1981) made a comparative study of Extroversion Neuroticism, Achievement motivation, adjustment of tribal, rural and urban youth of Himachal Pradesh. Through a stratified random sampling technique, 100 students from each area - tribal, Urban and rural were selected with an age range of 15 to 25 yrs from colleges of Himachal Pradesh. The Eysenek personality inventory (1964) and the Lynn achievement motivation questionnaire were used to administer the test. Some of the findings were (i) Sex emerged as a significant determinant of extraversion Neuroticism with means favoring females (ii) Urban males were higher on extraversion than tribal females.

Extraversion was negatively related to neuroticism and positively with the lie scale. (iii) In the case of rural youth extraversion, neuroticism was positively correlated with other variables. (iv) In case of urban youth Extroversion was negatively related to Neuroticism. (v) Neuroticism was not related with achievement motivation.

Srivastava (1982) made a comparative study of Neuroticism among male and female students during Adolescence - A comparative study. The objective were to (i) compare the level of neurotics among male and female adolescent students (ii) to compare the level of academic achievement of male and female adolescent student (iii) to find out differences in the level of neuroticism among male and female students with high and low academic achievement. The Kundur neurotic personality inventory was employed to collect data on neuroticism. The previous year academic annual examination marks were treated for academic achievement. The data were analyzed using frequency distribution, mean, standard deviation and t- test. The level of academic achievement was found to go down with the increase in the level of neuroticism among students.

Chatterji (1983) Studied the personality of arts, science, and commerce and agriculture students at the +2 stages was analyses using purposive and incidental sampling. 760 male students studying in 4 academic groups arts, Science, commerce and agriculture were selected as sample randomly. Eysenck's personality Inventory (EPI) used as a tool to measure personality of four groups of students. Group differences were noticed in extraversion, neuroticism, intelligence and achievement motivation.

Singh (1983) made an investigation on Social conformity in to some personality correlates (need achievement, Ned affiliation, Dominance, Extraversion, Neuroticism, Anxiety). Some hypotheses were (i) There isn’t significant correlation between conformity and extraversion and conformity and neuroticism. (ii) The relationship between conformity and extraversion and conformity and neuroticism is not affected by situational variations. The sample consisted of 400 male college students. Their age ranged from 16-23 years. Some of the findings were (i) there was a significant correlation between extraversion dimension of personality and conformity. (ii) The correlation of conformity with neuroticism was found to be insignificant. (iii) Extraversion and Neuroticism did not have a significant effect on conformity. The interaction between extraversion and situation was ineffective. This holds good in the cases of Neuroticism also.

Gupta (1985) studied personality characteristics of Bright and Dull children. Sample consists of 157 bright and 160 dull students studying in 12th Hindi Medium Secondary Schools in Luck now. Edwards's personal preference scheduled was used to test personality characteristic. There was significant difference among the bright and dull students.

Mitra (1985) studied some determinants of academic performance in preadolescent children, The objectives of the study were (i) to find out sex differences with regard to academic achievement, intelligence, achievement motivation, extraversion and neuroticism, (ii) to study the relationship between intelligence, achievement motivation, extraversion and neuroticism for both sexes. The sample consisted of 400 students, 200 boys and 200 girls, of classes IV to VII and age 9+ to 13+. The statistics used were the product-moment correlation and linear regression analysis. Extraversion positively and significantly correlated with academic achievement for both sexes. (iii) Students possessing relatively higher extraversion tended to achieve relatively higher, but neuroticism was not a factor that influenced achievement. (iv) There were no sex differences at the pre adolescent level with regard to intelligence, achievement motivation and extraversion, but the boys were more neurotic than the, girls.

Sathyagiri & Rajan (1985) conducted a study about the competency, personality, motivation and profession perception of college teachers. The major findings are: Teacher competency was related to intelligence, stability and conscientiousness tender mind, nature and placid nature, self-sufficiency. It was significantly related to creativity, dynamism, organized demeanors and warmth and self-actualization and profession perception of teachers. The more competent teacher significantly differed from the less competent teacher in all the above variables.

Sharma (1985) studied the nature and development of human personality in Ancient Indian thought. The objectives of the study were (i) To identify the enunciation of philosophical principles that conceptualized human personality in the various systems of ancient Indian thought.(ii) To undertake an exposition of the various constituents of human personality in each system. (iii) To assess the concept of human personality with a particular school of thought. (iv) To access the framework of the process of development of human personality in a particular school of thought. (v) To frame an integrated view of human personality. The study was philosophical-cum. historical. The sources used were Sutras and Bhasyas on the Indian school of thought as given in Vedas. The findings of the study. were (i) The composition of human personality in Vedanta was true to its metaphysical mainstay.

Human personality had only empirical existence Man's true personality was embedded in impersonality. (ii) Vedenta recommended four disciplines for the fullest development of human personality: discriminative knowledge, renunciation, the longing for liberation and ethical principles.

Wadhwa (1985) studied personality and attitude measures of Convent School teachers in relation to religion, religious fundamentalism and subject. This study deals with such a relationship between religious beliefs and two personality and two attitude measures in the Indian socio-cultural setting. A Catholic sample of 5 convent school Christian teachers was compared on neuroticism and extraversion measures of personality with 50 convent school Hindu teachers. Each sample was tested with 48 item Eyserck's Maudsley personality inventory, 20 item Christie's revised F-Scale and 40 item Rokeach Belief system scale. A 2X2X2 factorial design of analysis of variance for unequal cells was used to find the relationship between independent and dependent measures. Some of the findings were (i) Christian teachers were found to be less extroverted as compared to their Hindu counterparts. (ii) Hindu teachers teaching Humanities were found to be more neurotic as compared to the Hindu teachers teaching science.

Dandapani .C (1990) carried out an investigation of the neurotic tendencies in relation to SES and teaching success of Graduate Teacher in the higher sec. School of Mayuram taluk. The sample consists of nine hr. sec. schools. The tools of wood worth, Berrekuer scale were employed. The statistical method of the study in chi square. The findings were no relationship between the quality of teacher and neurotic tendencies.

Eysenck, Sybil, Kozeny and Jiri (1990) made cross cultural comparisons of personality on the students of Czech and English subjects. The sample was 419 male and 1496 female Czech and 1395 male and 1502 female U.K adults. Eysenck personality inventory was the tool used by them. Statistical procedure followed was factor analysis. Some of the major findings were (i) Czech students scored higher than their U.K. counterparts on Psychoticism and social desirability, but lower on Extroversion. (ii) Only females differed on Neuroticism with U.K. females securing higher than Czech females.

Singh D; Choudhury DR; Rao N P; Nayar S,(1990) in their study, Personality characteristic of teachers involved in the delivery of primary health care (Sevagram Experiment) An attempt was made to study the personality traits influencing the performance of 17 primary school teachers selected under ICMR project in Wardha district, to investigate feasibility and effectiveness of their involvement as primary health care workers vis-a-vis the 19 community health volunteers introduced by the State Government in the non-teacher villages of the project at the same time. The results indicated that both the teachers and community health volunteers preferred preventive and primitive health tasks and they showed no significant difference on the motivation and leadership orientation scale. The teachers, because of their job security and promotional avenues were satisfied with their achievements and were full of hopes and aspirations but the same was not true with the community health volunteers. This was due to their comparatively poor economic conditions and unstable source of livelihood.

Chitra et al, (1993) had noted a significant relationship between the independent variable personality (introversion-extroversion) and the dependent variable academic achievement of the SC respondents. The relationship between personality and academic achievement was stronger in SC respondents than their counter parts.

Raiszadesh Azar (1997) studied the relationship between personality type, learning style preference and mathematics achievement in college developmental mathematics. The primary objective was to investigate the relationship between student's personality types, learning style preferences and achievement in intermediate Algebra. Although the study showed no significant relationships between students personality types and their mathematics achievement in general. It was found that students with Intuition personality type achieved significantly higher mathematics scores than the students with sensing personality type. These differences along with indications from previous research have led this researcher to believe that learning style and personality type should be further investigated for their possible impact on students learning.

Barto (1998) found that there was a relationship between personality traits of sleeted New Jersey Public High School educators and Successful academic achievement of at risk students.

The Study by Cutchin (1998) showed relationship between the big five personality factors and performance criteria for in service high school teachers.

Sundaram, Subramanian and Vijaya (2002) had conducted a study on emotional intelligence and achievement of teacher trainees at primary level. The study reveals that the men and women teacher trainees do not differ in their emotional intelligence. The teacher trainees of government institutions are at a higher level that the teacher trainees of private institutions. The teacher trainees of co-education institutions are at a higher level than the teacher trainees in non co-education institutions in their EI. There is significant low positive correlation between emotional intelligence and total academic achievement.

Studies Related to Teaching Competency Done In India and Abroad:

2.3 Research Studies Related To Teaching Competency Conducted Abroad:

Gage (1960) stated, "Teaching skills are specific instructional techniques and procedures that a teacher may use in the classroom. They represent an analysis of the teaching process into relatively discrete components that can be used in different combination in the continuous flow of the teacher's performances".

Enos, D.F. (1976) had conducted a study on Cost Effectiveness Analysis of Competency based and non-competency based teacher education at San Diego State University, Austin. His finding was that competency-based teacher education trained teacher has outperformed graduates of the traditional programme. The trainees trained through micro teaching acquired higher general teaching competence as compared under traditional teacher education programme.

Larry, Darel Coulley, Braskamp A. and Frank Cossin (1979) in their study "Student rating and Instructor's self-ratings and that relationship to student Achievement", evaluated teaching over the following aspects of teaching viz., teacher support, student involvement, teacher skill and teacher control. The findings of the study confirmed that these few aspects constitute effective teaching through the discussion. The only significant predictor of class achievement was student ratings of teacher direction of the discussion.

Heng, May Hung and others (1997) had made a study on perception of teacher competence; from student to Teacher, in Hong Kong. The major finding was that both student teachers and beginning teachers perceived themselves as having higher competence in the classroom domain and lower in the school, community and professional domains

Chag Huaery-Por (1998) had conducted a study on the nature and assessment of teaching competency in apprentice science teachers in Taiwan. The major suggestion was that assessment of teaching competency from beginning teachers should be systematically collected and used for establishing the validity of teacher's evaluation instrument.

Carvello and Brienza (2001) had conducted a detailed study to find out if there is any relationship between emotional competence and leadership excellence. The study was conducted on 350 managers across the Johnson and Johnson Consumer Companies (JJCC) globally to assess if there are specific leadership competencies that distinguish high performs from average performers. Result showed that the highest performing managers have significantly more emotional competence than other managers.

A. A Adediwura and Bada Tayo (2007) in their study, perception of teachers' knowledge, and attitude and teaching skills as predictor of academic performance in Nigerian secondary schools, they investigated the relationship/effect of students' perception of teachers' knowledge of subject matter, attitude to work and teaching skills on students' academic performance. The population consisted of senior secondary three (SS.III) students in the South West Nigeria senior secondary schools. The result show that students' perception of teachers' knowledge of subject matter, attitude to work and teaching skills has a significant relationship on students' academic performance.

Christopher R. Gareis (2007) in his study to provide equal and equitable educational opportunity to all students. However, our focus on summative accountability measures often has an eclipsing effect on the equally important role of formative assessment practices in the classroom. This article describes *why* and *how* formative assessment should be integral to classroom teaching, and it suggests the importance of focusing on teachers' instructionally-based, formative assessment competencies through our teacher evaluation systems.

2.4 Research Studies Related To Teaching Competency Conducted In India

Kumar, Y & Lal, R. (1980) had conducted a study on effectiveness of micro teaching in improving general teaching competence of in-service teachers. They found that there was improvement in general teaching competence after undergoing training through micro teaching.

Sharma, S.K. (1981) analyzed the various relationships of teaching effectiveness in terms of competency. In the study, 220 classroom teaching-learning situations were observed; 2340 pupils respond to the questionnaire which assessed students linking of the teacher's teaching behavior. An achievement test was administered to

766 pupils of IX grade. The data was analyzed by employing principal component method of factor analysis and analysis of covariance. The finding of the study was there was no significant relationship between the age of the Hindi teachers, their attitude, interest and intelligence and their teaching competency.

Naik, V.V (1984) had made a comparative study of micro teaching and conventional approach of teaching training upon pupil's perception and general teaching competence of pre-service student teacher, found that there is no significant difference in the gain scores of general teaching competence of student teacher trained in micro teaching and conventional teacher training programme.

Sathyagiri, Rajan S. (1985) conducted a study about the competency, personality, motivation and profession perception of college teachers. The major findings are, teacher competency was related to intelligence, stability and conscientiousness tender mind , nature and placid nature, self-sufficiency. It was significantly related to creativity, dynamism, organized demeanors and warmth and self-actualization and profession perception of teachers. The more competent teacher significantly differed from the less competent teacher in all the above variables.

Singh, N. (1985) had conducted a study on Comparative study of Teacher Trained through Integrated and Traditional method in terms of attitude toward Teaching, Teaching Competence and Role Performance. The major findings were that there is no difference in the attitude of the groups under the two modes, there are differences in teaching competence and role performance and the integrated group scoring higher than the traditional group.

Thakkar, R. (1985) had conducted a study on the effect of different micro teaching skills upon General Teaching Competency of primary Teacher Trainees. He established that there is a significant positive effect of different micro teaching skills upon the general teaching competence of primary teacher training as measured by GTC scale.

Prakasham (1986) had made a study on teacher effectiveness as a function of school organization climate and Teaching competency. The sample consisted of 800 teachers teaching in classes IX, X, XI of different higher secondary schools. Employing the school organizational climate description questionnaire collected data by Moti Lal Sharma, the general teaching competency scale by B.K. Passi and M.L. Lalitha and the teacher effectiveness scale by Parmod Kumar. .Mean, T-values, coefficient of correlation, ANOVA and F-ratio's were computed for analyzing the data. The objectives of the study were to study the effect of school organizational climate on teacher effectiveness. The findings of their study were a positive and significant relationship was observed in the teacher effectiveness and teaching competency of teachers in different types of organizational climate.

Atreya, Jai Shankar (1989) had conducted a study of teacher's values in relation to their teaching effectiveness at degree-college level. The sample consisted of 600 teachers and was selected through random sampling. The tools used for the study were a new test for studying of values by Gilane; the teacher's effectiveness scale. The data were treated with't' test, partial correlation and multiple correlation. The objectives of the study were to identify teachers of high average, and low teaching effectiveness. The findings were that at the degree-level teaching effectiveness was significantly related to values and teaching satisfaction. Teaching effectiveness was found to be a normally distributed.

Vasanthi and Anandhi (1997) made an attempt to study the factors affecting Teacher Effectiveness of B.Ed. student-teachers. It was found that the factor of intelligence had high positive relation with Teacher Effectiveness among the B.Ed. students. The factor of intelligence has been found to be 51%. The positive correlation indicated that higher the intelligence the better was the Teacher Effectiveness as perceived by the teacher educators. It was found that among the made student teachers, the inner-correlation matrix showed a significant correlation between teacher effectiveness, intelligence and achievement-motivation, 40% attributed by intelligence while achievement-motivation, self-concept, attitude towards teaching and anxiety contributed negligibly. The inter-correlation matrix of women B.Ed., student-teachers, intelligence, self-concept and attitude towards teaching were found to be significantly correlated in the positive direction with teacher effectiveness.

Behera (2004) had conducted a study among the college teachers. The study that there is a significant positive relationship between teacher's effectiveness and emotional intelligence of junior college teachers as a whole and with various dimensions of teacher effectiveness.

Parveen Sharma (2005) in his research, Study of Teaching Aptitude in Relation to General Teaching Competency, Professional Teaching and Academic Achievements of B. Ed. Pupil Teachers, the objectives is to study the relationship among Teaching Aptitude (TA), General Teaching Competence (GTC), Professional Interest (PI) and Academic Achievement (AA) of B.Ed. pupil teachers. The findings are discipline and Sex of the pupil teachers does not contribute towards teaching aptitude of male and female arts pupil teachers were compared, it was observed that female arts pupil teachers secured significantly higher mean scores than their counterpart male arts pupil teacher. t was found that teaching aptitude of the pupil teacher was significantly correlated with their general teaching competence, professional interest and academic achievements. General teaching competence and professional interest of the pupil teachers significantly affect their teaching aptitude. In addition to this, effect of academic achievement on teaching aptitude of the pupil teaches was positive but not significant at acceptable level of confidence.

Viswanathappa. G. (2005) conducted a study in Anantapur district of Andhra Pradesh, to find out the influence of attitude towards teaching and teaching competence of student teachers at secondary of 200 student teachers. Tools employed were Attitude towards teaching profession developed by B.N. panda and S.C. panda (1998) and teaching competence scale developed by Viswanatan and Venkataiah (1992). The findings were that attitude towards Teaching plays a significant role in predicting the teaching competence of student teachers.

Xavier, S.A. and Amalraj, A. (2005) studied the teaching competency and its dimensions in postgraduate chemistry teachers working in the higher secondary schools of Kannyakumari District, Tamil Nadu. A teaching rating scale was constructed and validated by the investigator. The data were collected from 89 higher secondary postgraduate chemistry teachers. Using their scores in teaching competency and its dimensions, chemistry teachers were classified in to high, average and low teachers as regards competency.

2.5 Synthesis of Review of Related Literature:

The studies related to personality and Teaching competency done in abroad and India reveals that Beck(1967); Coats (1967); Murray (1972); Ekstrom's (1976); Carlyn, (1976); Duch, (1982);Liu (1983), Khan (1987), Dandapani C (1990), Cutchin, Gregery Charles (1998):, Sundaram, Subramanian and Vijaya (2002), Tracy Kitchel, Dr. Robert M. Torres, (2005) Jan Vopalensky (2007)) had done studies in personality, intelligence and achievement in different subjects among student-teachers.

Naik V.V (1984), Thakkarai 1985 and Gupta Suma (1991), Carvello and Brienza (2001), Sundaram, Subramanian and Vijayan (2002), Behera (2004) P. Anna raja and J. Sangeetha (2005) and G.

Viswanathappa(2005), Adediwura and Bada Tayo(2007), Christopher R. Gareis (2007) had done studies on general teaching competency among student-teachers.

A research gap is found from the above studies that attempts have been made previously to study the different aspects of personality and teaching competency separately. No one has attempted until now, to investigate the correlation between personality and teaching competency. To fill this research gap the investigator has taken the present study, "A study on Personality and Teaching Competency of B.Ed. Student Teachers".

3 Chapter

DESIGN OF THE STUDY

3.0 Methodology:

The methodology of the present investigation has been described under the following heads.

(i) Research method.

(ii) Sample of the study.

(iii) Tools used in the study.

(iv) Administration and scoring procedures of the tools.

(v) Statistical Techniques used.

3.1 Research Method:

The normative survey method is used in research to describe the problem or phenomenon. Survey method describes and interprets what exists at present. They are concerned with existing conditions or relations, prevailing practices, believes, attitudes, ongoing process and the emerging trends. Such investigations are variously termed in research literature as Descriptive Survey, Normative Survey, Status Studies or Trend Analysis. The term 'survey' and 'status' suggest the gathering of evidence relating to prevailing conditions. The term 'normative survey' is generally used for the type of research, which proposes to ascertain what is normal or typical condition or practice at the present time The normative survey was found to be best suited for the present study as the investigator was primarily concerned with the conditions and relationship which existed at that time. The present study aims at identifying the relationship between personality and teaching competency. Normative method deals with relatively a large number of cases in a particular time and gives generalized results. All these considerations led the investigator to use the normative survey method for her study.

3.2 Sample of the Study:

The present investigation was carried out in three B.Ed. colleges of Puducherry namely Immaculate College of Education, Pakamudayanpet, Loyola College of Education, Koodapakkam and Venkadeswara College of Education, Puducherry randomly. The investigator selected the colleges using stratified random sampling techniques, with due representation given to the variables viz.. sex (male and female), subject specification (science & arts), locality of the residence (rural & urban), school medium of instruction (Tamil & English), type of admission (CENTAC&CET), type of college (Government & Private), educational qualification, teaching experience, (experienced & inexperienced), parents educational qualifications (father & mother), The sample consisted of 84 males and 219 female trainees. Teacher Educators of these selected colleges observed their students using the tool (Appendix C).

3.3 Tools Used in the Study:

In this section, the details of the tools used for the collection of data are presented. The relevant variables for which the tools used are,

i) Maudsley Personality Inventory by H.J. Eysenck
ii) General Teaching Competency Scale (GTCS)
iii) Personal Information sheet

3.4 Description of the Tools:

a) Maudsley Personality Inventory by H.J. Eysenck:

Maudsley Personality Inventory (MPI) was designed to give a measure of two important personality characteristics such as Extroversion and Neuroticism. It consists of 48 questions in each of the traits. The traits were measures by means of 24 questions with two options 'Yes' and 'No'. The student has to encircle any one of the options. The investigator checks if all the 48 questions have been answered. The completed questionnaire was scrutinized for its scoring. Right responses were marked as "2" and wrong answers as "0". The total scoring Extroversion items gives scores of Extroversion and the total Neuroticism items gives scores of neuroticism. The tool is given in Appendix (B).

b) General Teaching Competency Scale (GTCS) developed by B.K. Passi and M.S. Lalitha (1979):

GTC scale is a classroom observation schedule. There are 21 items related to 21 teaching skills which encompass the entire teaching learning process in the classroom teaching namely, planning, presentation, closing, evaluation and managerial. The items are such that they are centered on teacher's classroom behavior in relation to pupil behavior. It is a 7 point rating scale measuring the use of the skill by the teacher in the classroom corresponding to each item ranging from for "not at all" to "7" for "very much". The GTC scale can be used to measure teaching competency of any teacher irrespective of age, sex, religion, socio-economic strata, grade level, and subject, rural/urban and so on. It can be used to train teachers both at pre-service and in-service level. A teacher can use the tool for self evaluation purpose also. The scale has been widely used not only by researches for doctoral studies (Parsi, 19977; Joshi, 1977) but also in the national projects undertaken by the National Council of Educational Research and Training. The actual score is 147; but for convenience the investigator has converted it to 100.

Therefore the score secured by the individual in the Teaching Competency is considered as the index of his/her Teaching Competency. The tool is given in Appendix (C).

c) Personal Information Sheet (Bio-Data) developed by the Researcher:

Before administering the personality tool, the investigator collected the necessary information related to the study by distributing personal information sheet. She gave appropriate instructions in order to make the information accurate. The specimen personal information sheet used in the study is given in Appendix (A)

3.5 Administration and Scoring Procedure of the Tools:

The tools were administered to the B.Ed. student teachers of the college of education concerned. It was administered during the practice teaching i.e. from October to June 2007. The investigator herself visited the colleges and individually distributed the tools with the personal information sheet to collect data regarding the variables. Before administering the scale the investigator implored the student, student teachers to extent their cooperation and assured that the information will be kept strictly confidential and will be used only for research purpose. The student-teachers were requested to go through the instructions given in the booklet, to read each statement carefully in the booklet and give their response in the answer sheet. Only 15minutes were given to answer the questionnaire. Assurance was given that the results would be used only for the research purpose and would not be revealed to others.

3.6 Scoring Procedure:

Scoring is done with the help of scoring key. The sum of ratings of all the items constitutes the score of trainees. According to the manual of the tool, the maximum possible score for each characteristics of personality is 48 and the minimum is 0, by comparing the means of neuroticism scores and extraversion scores, the level of personality of B.Ed. students are identified.

The maximum score for GTCS is 147 and the minimum is 21. The investigator has converted each individual score for 100. Therefore the score secured by the individual out of 100 in the Teaching Competency is considered as the index of his/her Teaching Competency. The scores are interpreted according to the points secured by the trainees.

3.7 Statistical Techniques Used:

The data collected by the investigator from the sample were analyzed statistically. In the present study the relevant data collected were the scores secured by 303 B.Ed. student teachers in personality Test and Teaching Competency Scales. These data were analyzed by employing the following statistical tools to arrive at meaningful conclusions.

i) Descriptive analysis
ii) Differential analysis
iii) Correlational analysis

i) Descriptive analysis:

It provides information about the nature of a particular group of individuals. To compare the two main groups mean and standard deviations were calculated. The essential descriptive statistics served as inputs for further inferential analysis. In the present investigation mean and standard deviation scores were calculated from the student's scores in Maudsley Personality Inventory and. General Teaching Competency Scale.

ii) Differential analysis:

It provides inferences involving determination of statistical significance of difference between groups with reference to the selected variable. In the present study,'t' value was calculated to test the significant difference between the mean scores of Maudsley Personality Inventory and Teaching Competency.

The't' test is a numerical procedure that marks the size of a mean difference between two groups, the number of subjects in each group and the amount of spread present in the scores. Thus The't' test is a technique used to determine whether the mean performance of the groups are significantly different or not. A significant value is a criterion used in making decision about the hypothesis.

The't' value was calculated by using the formula:

$$t = \frac{x_1 - x_2}{\sqrt{\frac{S_1{}^2}{N_1} + \frac{S_2{}^2}{N_2}}}$$

For variables with more than two such groups, to find the significant different between the groups 'F' analysis is the suitable technique.

iii) Correlation analysis:

Correlational analysis is used to find out the relationship between two variables. The correlation coefficient is valuable in the field of education as a measure of relationship between test scores and other measures of performance.

In the present study, correlation coefficient was used to find the relationship between test scores and other measures of performance.

$$r = \frac{n(\Sigma xy) - (\Sigma x)(\Sigma y)}{\sqrt{[n(\Sigma x^2) - (\Sigma x)^2]\,[n(\Sigma y^2) - (\Sigma y)^2]}}$$

In the present study, correlation coefficient was used to find the relationship between personality and Teaching Competency of B.Ed. student teachers.

4 Chapter

ANALYSIS AND INTERPRETATION

4.0 Introduction:

The present chapter deals with analysis and interpretations of the data which the investigator collected on the implementation of the tools of research. Analysis of data means studying the tabulated material in order to determine inherent facts or meanings. It is a process which involves breaking down existing complex factors into simple parts and putting the parts together in new arrangements for the purpose of interpretation of the statistical techniques, which are necessary for the purpose of the study and presents the results in an organized and meaningful form.

The process of interpretation is essentially one of stating what the results are, what they mean, what their significance is and what the answer to the original problem is. This process calls for a critical examination of the results of one's analysis in the light of his/her previous analysis concerning collection of data.

In accordance with the objectives of the present study, the data were gathered, tabulated, classified and analyzed systematically and objectively. The study involved on variables namely personality and Teaching competency and other such variables such as sex, educational qualifications, subject, type of admission, type of college, medium of instruction, locality, and father's educational qualification.

4.1 Scheme of Analysis:

According to Fergusin F.A. (1981) "The process of interpretation is essentially what the results show, what do they mean, what is their significance and what is the answer to the original problem".

Interpretation is the most important step in the total procedure of research. It calls for a critical examination of the limitations of the data gathered and its subjective attitude. To avoid subjectivity one must be critical in one's own thinking and must have adequate knowledge of techniques of research.

In the present study, the relevant data collected were the scores secured by the B.Ed. student teachers of the Colleges of Education, in Puducherry. The data collected by the investigator from the sample were analyzed statistically.

Level of Significance:

All the hypotheses formulated in this study were studied and tested and testing hypothesis were done on the basis of results obtained through the analysis of data using statistical procedure and the level of significance for rejection or acceptance of the hypotheses has to be decided in advance. In reporting the findings of the study, the researcher indicates the actual probability level associated with the findings, so that; the reader may have his own judgment in deciding whether the null hypotheses should be rejected or accepted. In the present study, 0.05 level of significance has been taken into account. The data was thus statistically treated and results are presented in the following pages.

Table 1:
Mean Median, Mode and Standard Deviation of Personality scores of B.Ed. student teachers

Personality	No	Mean	Median	Mode	S.D.
Neuroticism	303	25.47	26	32	8.25
Extraversion	303	27.98	28	28	5.30

From the table 1, the mean and standard deviation of B.Ed. student teachers are computed to be 25.47, 8.25 respectively for Neuroticism and 27.98, 5.30 respectively for Extraversion. According to the manual of the tool, the maximum possible score for each characteristics of personality is 48 and the minimum is 0, by comparing the means of neuroticism scores and extraversion scores, B.Ed. students are extrovert.

Hypothesis 1: The level of teaching competency of B.Ed. student teacher is high.

Table 2:
Mean, Median, Mode and Standard Deviation of Teaching Competency scores of B.Ed. student teachers

	No	Mean	Median	Mode	Standard Deviation
Teaching competency	303	73.12	75	80	10.41

The mean, median, mode and the standard deviation of teaching competency scores of B.Ed. student teachers are computed to be 73.12, 75, 80 and 10.41 respectively. According to the manual of the tool, the maximum possible score for teaching competency is 147 and the minimum is 21. The teaching competency of B.Ed. student teachers is just above average. Hence, the hypothesis is rejected.

Hypothesis 2: There is no significant relationship between extraversion and teaching competency of the B.Ed. student teachers.

Table 3:
The Correlation coefficient between Extraversion and Teaching competency

Variable	N	Teaching Competency	Level of Significance (0.05)
Extraversion	303	r = 0.05	NS
Teaching competency	303		

From the table 3 the calculated value 0.05 is lesser than the 'r' table value. Therefore, there is no significant relationship between extraversion and teaching competency. Hence the hypothesis is accepted.

Hypothesis 3: There is no significant relationship between Neuroticism and teaching competency of the B.Ed. student teachers.

Table 4:
The Correlation coefficient between Neuroticism and Teaching competency

Variable	N	Teaching Competency	Level of Significance (0.05)
Neuroticism	303	r = -0.203	S
Teaching competency	303		

From the table 4 the calculated value -0.203 is greater than the 'r' table value. Therefore, there is significant relationship between Neuroticism and Teaching competency. Hence the hypothesis is rejected.

Hypothesis 4: There is no significant difference between the mean scores of Neuroticism scores of male and female B.Ed. student teachers.

Table 5:
Mean, Standard deviation, Mean difference and't' value of Neuroticism scores of male and female B.Ed. student teachers

Variable	Subject Groups	N	Mean	S.D.	Mean difference	't' value	Level of significance (0.05)
Sex	Male	84	27.45	7.15	2.74	2.62	S
	Female	219	24.71	8.53			

From the Table 5, it is found that the mean difference 2.74 between the mean scores of Neuroticism of B.Ed. student teachers is significant at 0.05 level of significance. Hence, the null hypothesis is rejected. But there is difference in their mean, i.e. male student teachers is better than female.

Hypothesis 5: There is no significant difference between the mean scores of Extraversion scores of male and female B.Ed. student teachers

Table 6:
Mean, Standard deviation, Mean difference and't' value of scores Extraversion of male and female B.Ed. student teachers

Variable	Subject Groups	N	Mean	S.D.	Mean difference	't' value	Level of significance(0.05)
sex	Male	84	27.67	5.29			
	Female	219	28.10	5.31	0.43	0.64	NS

From the Table 6, it is found that the mean difference 0.43 between the mean scores Extraversion of B.Ed. student teachers is not significant at 0.05 level of significance. Hence, the null hypothesis is accepted. But there is difference in their mean, i.e. female student teachers is better than male.

Hypothesis 6: There is no significant difference between the mean scores of the Neuroticism scores of B.Ed. student teachers who had studied in Tamil medium and English medium at the school level.

Table 7:
Comparison of Neuroticism scores of English and Tamil medium at the school level of the B.Ed. student teachers

Variable	Subject Groups	N	Mean	S.D.	Mean difference	't' value	Level of significance (0.05)
Medium of the school	English	64	22.41	6.68			
	Tamil	238	26.26	8.46	3.86	3.38	S

From the Table 7, the mean difference between the mean scores of B.Ed. trainees whose medium of instruction at the school level were English and Tamil is computed to be 3.86. As the calculated't' value 3.38 is greater than the table value 1.96 at 0.05 level of significance, the null hypothesis is rejected.

Hypothesis 7: There is no significant difference between the mean scores of the Extraversion scores of B.Ed. student teachers who had studied in Tamil medium and English medium at the school level.

Table 8:
Comparison of Extraversion scores of English and Tamil medium at the school level of the B.Ed. student teachers

Variable	Subject Groups	N	Mean	S.D.	Mean difference	't' value	Level of significance(0.05)
Medium of the school	English	64	27.80	5.17	0.23	0.31	NS
	Tamil	238	28.03	5.36			

From the Table 8, the mean difference between the mean scores of B.Ed. trainees whose medium of instructions at the school level were English and Tamil is computed to be 0.23. As the calculated't' value 0.31 is less than the table value 1.96 at 0.05 level of significance, the null hypothesis is accepted.

Hypothesis 8: There is no significant difference between the mean scores of the Neuroticism scores of B.Ed. student teachers who had admitted through CENTAC and CET.

Table 9:
Comparison between the Neuroticism scores of B.Ed. student teachers who had admitted through CENTAC and CET

Variable	Groups	N	Mean	S.D.	Mean difference	't' value	Level of significance(0.05)
Type of Admission	CET	231	25.68	8.65			
	CENTAC	72	24.79	6.84	0.89	0.80	N.S.

From the Table 9, it is found that the mean difference 0.89 between the Neuroticism scores of B.Ed. student teachers who had admitted through CENTAC and CET is found to be not significant. The't' value 0.08. is less than the table value 1.96 at 0.05 level of significance. Hence, the null hypothesis is accepted.

Hypothesis 9: There is no significant difference between the mean scores of the Extraversion scores of B.Ed. student teachers who had admitted through CENTAC and CET.

Table 10:
Comparison between the Extraversion scores of B.Ed. student teachers who had admitted through CENTAC and CET

Variable	Groups	N	Mean	S.D.	Mean difference	't' value	Level of significance(0.05)
Type of Admission	CET	231	27.88	5.38			
	CENTAC	72	28.29	5.07	0.41	0.57	N.S.

From the Table 10 it is found that the mean difference 0.41between Extraversion scores of B.Ed. student teachers who had admitted through CENTAC and CET is found to be not significant. The't' value 0.57 is less than the table value 1.96 at 0.05 level of significance. Hence, the null hypothesis is accepted.

Hypothesis 10: There is no significant difference between the mean scores of the Neuroticism scores of B.Ed. student teachers who had studied in private colleges and government colleges.

Table 11:
Comparison of Neuroticism scores of B.Ed. student teachers who had studied in private and government colleges

Variable	Subject Groups	N	Mean	S.D.	Mean difference	't' value	Level of significance(0.05)
Type of College	Private	170	25.34	8.28	0.21	0.22	N.S.
	Government	133	25.59	8.24			

From the Table 11, the mean difference between the mean scores of Neuroticism scores of B.Ed. student teachers who had studied in Private and Government colleges is found to be 0.21. This mean difference is found to be not significant as the calculated't' value 0.22 is less than the table value 1.96 at 0.05 level of significance. The null hypothesis is accepted.

Hypothesis 11: There is no significant difference between the mean scores of the Extraversion scores of B.Ed. student teachers who had studied in private colleges and government colleges.

Table 12:
Comparison of Extraversion scores of B.Ed. student teachers who had studied in private and government colleges

Variable	Subject Groups	N	Mean	S.D.	Mean difference	't' value	Level of significance(0.05)
Type of College	Private	170	27.98	4.98	0.01	0.01	N.S.
	Government	133	27.97	5.71			

From the Table 12, the mean difference between the mean scores of Extraversion of B.Ed. student teachers who had studied in

Private and Government colleges is found to be 0.01 This mean difference is found to be not significant as the calculated't' value 0.01is less than the table value 1.96 at 0.05 level of significance. The null hypothesis is accepted.

Hypothesis 12: There is no significant difference in the mean scores of Neuroticism scores of Science and Arts group of B.Ed. student teachers.

Table13:
Neuroticism scores of Science and Arts group of B.Ed.student teachers

Variable	Subject Groups	N	Mean	S.D.	Mean difference	't' value	Level of significance(0.05)
Subject Specialization	Arts	120	26.19	8.50	1.20	1.24	N.S.
	Science	123	24.99	8.07			

From the table 13 it is found that the mean difference 1.20 between Neuroticism scores of B.Ed. student teachers of science and arts group is found not to be significant. The calculated't' value 1.24 is less than the table value 1.96 at 0.05 level of significance. Hence, the null hypothesis is accepted.

Hypothesis 13: There is no significant difference in the mean scores of Extraversion scores **of** Science and Arts group of B.Ed. student teachers.

Table 14:
Extraversion scores of Science and Arts group of B.Ed. Student teachers

Variable	Subject Groups	N	Mean	S.D.	Mean difference	't' value	Level of significance(0.05)
Subject specialization	Arts	120	27.92	5.31	0.11	0.17	N.S.
	Science	123	28.02	5.31			

From the table 14, it is found that the mean difference is 0.11 between Extraversion scores of B.Ed. student teachers of science and arts group is found not to be significant. The calculated't' value 0.17 is less than the table value 1.96 at 0.05 level of significance. Hence, the null hypothesis is accepted.

Hypothesis 14: There is no significant difference between the mean scores of the Neuroticism scores in the Educational qualification of B.Ed. student teachers.

Table 15:
Neuroticism scores of Postgraduate and Undergraduate B.Ed. student teachers

Variable	Subject Groups	N	Mean	S.D.	Mean differ rence	't' value	Level of significa nce(0.05)
Educational Qualification	Postgra-duate	73	23.85	9.12			
	Under graduate	230	25. 67	7.97	0.82	0.74	N.S.

From the Table 15, the mean difference 0.82 between the mean scores of Neuroticism of B.Ed. student teachers whose educational qualification are postgraduate and undergraduate is found not to be significant. The calculated't' value 0.74 less than the table value 1.96 at 0.05 level of significance. Hence the null hypothesis is accepted.

Hypothesis 15: There is no significant difference between the mean scores of the Extraversion scores in the Educational qualification of B.Ed. student teachers.

Table 16:
Extraversion scores of Postgraduate and Undergraduate B.Ed. student teachers

Variable	Subject Groups	N	Mean	S.D.	Mean differe nce	't' value	Level of significan ce(0.05)
Educational Qualification	Postgrad uate	73	28.78	5.49			
	Under-graduate	230	27.73	5.23	1.05	1.48	N.S.

From the Table 16, the mean difference 1.05 between the mean scores of Extraversion of B.Ed. student teachers whose educational qualification are Postgraduate and Undergraduate is found not to be significant. The calculated't' value 1.48 is less than the table value 1.96 at 0.05 level of significance. Hence the null hypothesis is accepted.

Hypothesis 16: There is no significant difference between the mean scores of the Neuroticism scores of B.Ed. student teachers who have teaching experience and those who do not have teaching experience.

Table 17:
Neuroticism scores of those who have teaching experience and those who do not have teaching experience of B.Ed. student teachers

Variable	Subject Groups	N	Mean	S.D.	Mean difference	't' value	Level of significance(0.05)
Teaching experience	Experience	31	25.16	10.84			
	Inexperience	272	25.50	7.93	0.34	0.22	N.S

The mean difference 0.34 between the mean scores of Neuroticism of B.Ed. student teachers who have teaching experience and who do not have teaching experience is found not to be significant. The calculated't' value 0.22 is less than the table 't' value 1.96 at 0.05 level of significance. Hence, the null hypothesis is accepted.

Hypothesis 17: There is no significant difference between the mean scores of the Extraversion scores of B.Ed. student teachers who have teaching experience and those who do not have teaching experience.

Table 18:
Extraversion scores of those who have teaching experience and those who do not have teaching experience of B.Ed. student teachers

Variable	Subject Groups	N	Mean	S.D.	Mean difference	't' value	Level of significance(0.05)
Teaching experience	Experience	31	28.71	6.08			
	Inexperience	272	27.90	5.21	0.81	0.81	N.S

From the Table 18, the mean difference 0.81 between the mean scores of Extraversion scores of B.Ed. student teachers who have teaching experience and who do not have teaching experience is found not to be significant. The calculated't' value 0.81 is less than the table't' value 1.96 at 0.05 level of significance. Hence, the null hypothesis is accepted.

Hypothesis 18: There is no significant difference between the mean scores of the Neuroticism scores of B.Ed. student teachers who had studied in urban and rural students.

Table 19:
Comparison between the Neuroticism scores of Urban and Rural B.Ed. student teachers

Variable	Subject Groups	N	Mean	S.D.	Mean difference	't' value	Level of significance (0.05)
Locality of Residence	Urban	193	25.53	7.49	0.18	0.18	NS
	Rural	110	25.35	9.47			

From the table 19, the mean difference 0.81 between the mean scores of Neuroticism scores of students who belong to urban and rural area is found not to be significant. The calculated't' value 0.18 is less than the table value 1.96 at 0.05 level of significance. Hence the null hypothesis is accepted.

Hypothesis 19: There is no significant difference between the mean scores of the Extraversion scores of B.Ed. student teachers who had studied in urban and rural students.

Table 20:
Comparison between the Extraversion scores of Urban and Rural B.Ed. student teachers

Variable	Subject Groups	N	Mean	S.D.	Mean difference	't' value	Level of significance (0.05)
Locality of Residence	Urban	193	27.65	5.11	0.90	1.43	NS
	Rural	110	28.55	5.60			

From the table 20, the mean difference 0.90 between the mean scores of Extraversion **scores** of students who belong to urban and rural area is found not to be significant. The calculated't' value 1.43 is less than the table value 1.96 at 0.05 level of significance. Hence the null hypothesis is accepted.

Hypothesis 20: There is no significant difference between the mean scores of the Neuroticism scores of B.Ed. student teachers with regard to the variable parental educational qualification.

Table 21:

Comparison of Neuroticism scores of Student teachers with regard to their Father's educational qualification

Variable	Sources of variation	Sum of squares	D.f.	Mean Square	F	Level of significance (0.05)
Father's qualification	Between groups	200.36	4	50.09	0.73	NS
	Within groups	20355.09	298	68.31		
	Total	20555.45	302			

From the table 21, it is observed that the father's qualification is not found to be significant, the mean difference between the subgroups of Neuroticism score. The 'F' value 0.73 is less than table value at 0.05 level of significance, so the null hypothesis is accepted.

Hypothesis 21: There is no significant difference between the mean scores of the Extraversion scores of B.Ed. student teachers with regard to the variable parental educational qualification.

Table 22:
Comparison of the Extraversion scores of Student teachers with regard to their Father's educational qualification

Variable	Sources of variation	Sum of squares	D.f.	Mean Square	F	Level of significance (0.05)
Father's qualification	Between groups	125.85	4	31.46	0.35	NS
	Within groups	8364.03	298	28.07		
	Total	8489.88	302			

From the table 21, it is observed that the father's qualification is not found to be significant in the mean difference between the subgroups of Extraversion score. The 'F' value 0.35 is less than the table value at 0.05 level of significance, so the null hypothesis is accepted.

Hypothesis 22: There is no significant difference between the mean scores of the teaching competency scores of male and female B.Ed. student teachers.

Table 23:
Comparison of Teaching Competency scores of male and female of B.Ed. student teachers

Variable	Subject Groups	N	Mean	S.D.	Mean difference	't' value	Level of significance (0.05)
Sex	Male	84	69.95	10.66	4.38	3.33	S
	Female	219	74.33	10.08			

From the table 23, the mean difference 4.38 between the male and female B.Ed. student teachers in teaching competency scores is found to be significant .As the calculated't' value 3.33 is greater than the table value 1.96 at 0.05 level of significance, the null hypothesis is rejected.

Hypothesis 23: There is no significant difference between the mean scores of the teaching competency scores of B.Ed. student teachers whose medium of instruction at school level were English and Tamil.

Table 24:
Comparison of Teaching Competency scores of Medium of school of the B.Ed. student teachers

Variable	Subject Groups	N	Mean	S.D.	Mean difference	't' value	Level of significance (0.05)
Medium of School	English	64	77.02	10.48	2.16	3.47	S
	Tamil	238	72.02	10.15			

From the table 24, the mean difference 2.16 between the mean scores of teaching competency scores of B.Ed. student teachers whose medium of instructions at the school level is found to be significant. As the calculated't' value 3.47 is greater than the table value 1.96 at 0.05 level of significance, the null hypothesis is rejected.

Hypothesis 24: There is no significant difference between the mean scores of the teaching competency scores of B.Ed. student teachers who had admitted through CENTAC and CET.

Table 25:
Comparison between the Teaching Competency scores of B.Ed. student teachers who had who had admitted through CENTAC and CET

Variable	Subject Groups	N	Mean	S.D.	Mean difference	't' value	Level of significance(0.05)
Type of Admission	CET	231	73.03	9.88	0.37	0.27	NS
	CENTAC	72	73.40	12.05			

From the table 25, the mean difference 0.37 between the mean scores of Teaching Competency scores of B.Ed. student teachers who had admitted through CENTAC and CET is found not to be significant. As the calculated't' value is 0.27 is lesser than the table value 1.96 at 0.05 level of significance, the null hypothesis is accepted.

Hypothesis 25: There is no significant difference between the mean scores of the teaching competency scores of B.Ed. student teachers who had studied in private colleges and government colleges.

Table 26:
Comparison of the Teaching Competency scores of B.Ed. student teachers who had studied in private and government colleges

Variable	Subject Groups	N	Mean	S.D.	Mean difference	't' value	Level of significance(0.05)
Type of College	Private	170	72.61	9.94	1.16	0.96	N.S.
	Government	133	73.77	11.00			

From the table 26, the mean difference 1.16 between the teaching competency of private colleges and government colleges is found to be not significant. The calculated't' value 0.96 is less than the table value 1.96 at 0.05 level of significance. Hence, the null hypothesis is accepted.

Hypothesis 26: There is no significant difference in the mean scores of teaching competency scores of science and arts group of B.Ed. student teachers.

Table 27:
Comparison between the Teaching Competency scores of Science and Arts group of B.Ed. student teachers

Variable	Subject Groups	N	Mean	S.D.	Mean difference	't' value	Level of significance(0.05)
Subject specialization	Arts	120	72.51	12.45	1.01	0.83	N.S.
	Science	123	73.52	8.84			

From the table 27, the mean difference 1.01 between the teaching competency scores of science and arts group of B.Ed. student teachers is found to be not significant. The calculated't' value 0.83 is less than the table value 1.96 at 0.05 level of significance. Hence, the null hypothesis is accepted.

Hypothesis 27: There is no significant difference between the mean scores of the teaching competency scores of B.Ed. student teachers regarding the variable Educational qualification.

Table 28:
Teaching Competency scores of postgraduate and Undergraduate B.Ed. student teachers

Variable	Subject Groups	N	Mean	S.D.	Mean difference	't' value	Level of significance(0.05)
Educational qualification	Postgraduate	73	74.41	9.90	1.70	1.22	N.S.
	Undergraduate	230	72.71	10.56			

From the table 28, the mean difference 1.70 between the teaching competency of Postgraduate and Undergraduate teachers is found not to be significant. The calculated't' value 1.22 is less than the table value 1.96 at 0.05 level of significance. Hence the null hypothesis is accepted.

Hypothesis 28: There is no significant difference between the mean scores of the teaching competency scores of B.Ed. student teachers who have teaching experience and those who do not have teaching experience.

Table 29:
Teaching Competency scores of those who have teaching experience and those who do not have teaching experience of B.Ed. student teachers

Variable	Subject Groups	N	Mean	S.D.	Mean difference	't' value	Level of significance(0.05)
Teaching experience	Experience	31	72.94	10.83	0.20	0.10	N.S
	Inexperience	272	73.14	10.39			

From the table 29, the mean difference 0.20 between the mean scores of teaching competency scores of those who have experience and those who do not have experience is found not be significant. The calculated't' value 0.10 is less than the table value 1.96 at 0.05 level of significance. Therefore, the null hypothesis is accepted.

Hypothesis 29: There is no significant difference between the mean scores of the teaching competency scores of B.Ed. student teachers who had studied in urban and rural students.

Table 30:
Comparison between the teaching competency scores of Urban and Rural B.Ed. student teachers

Variable	Subject Groups	N	Mean	S.D.	Mean difference	't' value	Level of significance(0.05)
Locality of Residence	Urban	193	73.75	10.64	1.73	1.39	NS
	Rural	110	72.02	9.96			

From the table 30, the mean difference 1.73 between teaching competency of urban and rural students is found to be not significant. The calculated't' value 1.39 is less than the table value 1.96 at 0.05 level of significance. Hence, the null hypothesis is accepted.

Hypothesis 30: There is no significant difference between the mean scores of the teaching competency scores of B.Ed. student teachers with regard to the parent's educational qualification.

Table 31:
Comparison of Teaching Competency scores of Student teachers with regard to their Father's educational qualification

Variable	Sources of variation	Sum of squares	D.f	Mean Square	F	Level of significance (0.05)
Father's Educational qualification	Between groups	554.59	4	138.65	1.28	NS
	Within groups	32203.14	298	108.06		
	Total	32757.72	302			

From the table 31, the background variable Father's educational qualification has no significant mean difference between the subgroups in the teaching competency scores. The calculated 'F' value 1.28 is less than the table 'F' value at 0.05 level of significance. Hence, the null hypothesis is accepted.

5 Chapter

SUMMARY, MAJOR FINDINGS, DISCUSSION, CONCLUSION, RECOMMENDATION AND SUGGESTIONS FOR FURTHER RESEARCH

5.1 Need of the Study:

Teachers Personality and teaching competencies play an important role in teaching profession. In the midst of hectic life prevailing in the modern world, a teacher should have good personality and his/her teaching should be competent-based. If the teachers are competent and have balanced personality, the entire nation will be benefited.

The present centaury throws a number of challenges before the teachers. For working satisfactorily, the teachers should know how to adjust, how to manage the class, how to teach the students and how to contribute with full potential towards institutional goals as well as towards the welfare of the society and the nation at large. This is possible when the personality of the teacher trainee is properly molded. Unfortunately, our educational set up emphasis only on the cognitive aspect of the human resources, whereas the personality aspect of human resources is neglected. Personality factors are important, sometimes more than the academic competence. However good may be the system of education, curriculum and text books, if the teachers are not competent, education by and large will be ineffective. Therefore, the personality factors and teaching competency of the B.Ed. student's teachers play a vital role in their successful survival and fitness in the profession. Hence there is need for the present study.

5.2 Statement of the Problem:

"A study on personality and teaching competency of B.Ed. student teachers."

5.3 **Significance of the Problem:**

Healthy development of the individual and his personality may be regarded as one of the aims of education. Education has to be arranged that it helps the process of personality development. It is well know that teaching is influenced by personality characteristics of teacher. In the words of secondary education commission (1952-53), every teacher and educationalist of experiences knows that even the best curriculum and the perfect syllabus remains dead, unless quickened in to life by right methods of teaching and right kind of teachers. However good may be the system of education, curriculum and textbooks if the teachers are not efficient, competent and if the teachers are not well balanced in their personality then education by and large will be ineffective.

Teachers play an important role in the academic achievement of pupils. It is the responsibility of the teacher to make the pupils to grow in the full status in the overall development. Teacher should provide the necessary experiences and training to the pupil and ensure them to behave as per the expectations of society and lead a successful life. In order to succeed in such duties the teacher should be more efficient and alert.

The student teachers are at the threshold of entering into the career of teaching. Personality plays an important role in teaching profession. A student teacher should have good personality charters in the midst of hectic life prevailing in the modern world. The future of a nation depends upon the role played by the members of the teaching community. It is a pleasant privilege of the teacher, to shape the children of the nation into useful citizens of tomorrow. Therefore personality and teaching competency of the student teacher should be developed to face the growing, which in turn enhance their teaching performance.

Corey (1964) comments on the practicability of research as "No educational research project shall be undertaken unless its consequences give promise of improving significantly an important educational practice or operation".

By considering this is mind the present study was undertaken by the researcher to identify the level of personality characteristics and teaching competency of the student teachers. In the present study an attempt was made to find out the inner relationship among personality and teaching competency of B.Ed., student teachers. Definitely this study will lead to better understanding of the proper conditions for the maintenance of the good personality and teaching competency of the student teachers.

5.4 Objectives of the Study:

1. Primary Objectives:

i) To study the personality characteristics of B.Ed. student teachers.
ii) To study the level of teaching competency of B.Ed. student teachers.
iii) To study the relationship, if any, between the Neuroticism and teaching competency of B.Ed. student teachers.
iv) To study the relationship, if any, between the extraversion and teaching competency of B.Ed. student teachers.
v) To study the relationship, if any, between the Neuroticism and Extraversion of B.Ed. student teachers

2. Secondary Objectives:

1) To find out the difference, if any, between the groups in their personality of B.Ed. Student Teachers regarding the following background variables:

    i) Sex
    ii) Medium of the schools
    iii) Type of school studied
    iv) Type of college studied
    v) Subject specification
    vi) Educational qualification
    vii) Teaching experience
    viii) Locality of residence
    ix) Parents educational qualification

2) To find out the difference, if any, between the groups in their Teaching Competency of B.Ed. Student Teachers regarding the following background variables.

    i) Sex
    ii) Medium of the schools
    iii) Type of school studied
    iv) Type of college studied
    v) Subject specification
    vi) Educational qualification
    vii) Teaching experience
    viii) Locality of residence
    ix) Parents educational qualification

5.5 Hypotheses of the Study:

The hypotheses of the study formed in the light of objectives and review of related literature are as follows:

1) The level of teaching competency of B.Ed. student teacher is high.
2) There is no significant relationship between extraversion and teaching competency of the B.Ed. student teachers.
3) There is no significant relationship between Neuroticism and teaching competency of the B.Ed. student teachers.
4) There is no significant difference between the mean scores of Neuroticism scores of male and female B.Ed. student teachers.
5) There is no significant difference between the mean scores of Extraversion scores of male and female B.Ed. student teachers
6) There is no significant difference between the mean scores of the Neuroticism scores of B.Ed. student teachers who had studied in Tamil medium and English medium at the school level.
7) There is no significant difference between the mean scores of the Extraversion scores of B.Ed. student teachers who had studied in Tamil medium and English medium at the school level.
8) There is no significant difference between the mean scores of the Neuroticism scores of B.Ed. student teachers who had admitted through CENTAC and CET.
9) There is no significant difference between the mean scores of the Extraversion scores of B.Ed. student teachers who had admitted through CENTAC and CET.

10) There is no significant difference between the mean scores of the Neuroticism scores of B.Ed. student teachers who had studied in private colleges and government colleges.
11) There is no significant difference between the mean scores of the Extraversion scores of B.Ed. student teachers who had studied in private colleges and government colleges.
12) There is no significant difference in the mean scores of Neuroticism scores of Science and Arts group of B.Ed. student teachers.
13) There is no significant difference in the mean scores of Extraversion scores of Science and Arts group of B.Ed. student teachers.
14) There is no significant difference between the mean scores of the Neuroticism scores in the Educational qualification of B.Ed. student teachers.
15) There is no significant difference between the mean scores of the Extraversion scores in the Educational qualification of B.Ed. student teachers.
16) There is no significant difference between the mean scores of the Neuroticism scores of B.Ed. student teachers who have teaching experience and those who do not have teaching experience.
17) There is no significant difference between the mean scores of the Extraversion scores of B.Ed. student teachers who have teaching experience and those who do not have teaching experience.
18) There is no significant difference between the mean scores of the Neuroticism scores of B.Ed. student teachers who had studied in urban and rural students.

19) There is no significant difference between the mean scores of the Extraversion scores of B.Ed. student teachers who had studied in urban and rural students.

20) There is no significant difference between the mean scores of the Neuroticism scores of B.Ed. student teachers with regard to the variable parental educational qualification.

21) There is no significant difference between the mean scores of the Extraversion scores of B.Ed. student teachers with regard to the variable parental educational qualification.

22) There is no significant difference between the mean scores of the teaching competency scores of male and female B.Ed. student teachers.

23) There is no significant difference between the mean scores of the teaching competency scores of B.Ed. student teachers whose medium of instruction at school level were English and Tamil.

24) There is no significant difference between the mean scores of the teaching competency scores of B.Ed. student teachers who had admitted through CENTAC and CET.

25) There is no significant difference between the mean scores of the teaching competency scores of B.Ed. student teachers who had studied in private colleges and government colleges.

26) There is no significant difference in the mean scores of teaching competency scores of science and arts group of B.Ed. student teachers.

27) There is no significant difference between the mean scores of the teaching competency scores of B.Ed. student teachers regarding the variable Educational qualification.

28) There is no significant difference between the mean scores of the teaching competency scores of B.Ed. student teachers who

have teaching experience and those who do not have teaching experience.

29) There is no significant difference between the mean scores of the teaching competency scores of B.Ed. student teachers who had studied in urban and rural students.

30) There is no significant difference between the mean scores of the teaching competency scores of B.Ed. student teachers with regard to the parent's educational Qualification.

5.6 Description of the Study:

In order to achieve the objectives, normative survey method was used because the investigation was primarily concerned with the relationship between the two variables, namely personality and teaching competency. It also deals with relatively a large number of cases in a particular time. The various variables involved this study are personality, teaching competency, sex, educational qualification, locality of residence, subject specialization and parental qualification. The investigator has administered the tool only to B.Ed. students of the colleges of education in Puducherry region only. The sample of the study consists of 303 B.Ed. students studying in three colleges of education namely Immaculate College of Education, Loyola College of Education and Venkadeswara College of Education, Puducherry in the academic year 2006-07. All the available subjects were taken for this study. The student-teachers were categorized based on the optional subjects (science and arts) taken, qualification (UG/PG), sex (male/female), native location (urban/rural), college location (urban/rural), medium of instruction in school (English/Tamil), type of college last studied (Private/Govt.) and parent's qualification. The investigator has made use of the M.P.I tool used for personality, constructed and standardized by H.J. Eysenck, Professor of Psychology, University of London. The tool constructed By B.K. Passi and M.S. Lalitha was used for the General Teaching Competency Scale (GTCS). The raw data of the Personality and Teaching Competency were used for the statistical evaluation. The mean and standard deviation for the scores of Personality and teaching competency were calculated. Mean difference was found out and was used for testing the significant differences in Personality. Correlation was used to find the relationship between Personality and teaching competency.

5.7 Major Findings:

1. The teaching competency of the B.Ed. students is found to be just above average.
2. There is no significant relationship between extraversion and teaching competency of the B.Ed. student teachers.
3. There is significant relationship between Neuroticism and Teaching competency of the B.Ed. student teachers.
4. The mean difference is found to be significant between the male and female B.Ed. student teachers with Neuroticism
5. There is no significant difference between the mean scores of Extraversion. Scores of male and female B.Ed. student teachers.
6. There is significant difference between the mean scores of the Neuroticism scores of B.Ed. student teachers who had studied in Tamil medium and English medium at the school level.
7. There is no significant difference between the mean scores of the Extraversion scores of B.Ed. student teachers who had studied in Tamil medium and English medium at the school level.
8. There is no significant difference between the mean scores of the Neuroticism scores of B.Ed. student teachers who had admitted through CENTAC and CET.

9. There is no significant difference between the mean scores of Extraversion scores of B.Ed. student teachers who had admitted through CENTAC and CET
10. The private and Government college students do not differ significantly in their Neuroticism scores as their mean difference is not significant.
11. The private and Government college students do not differ significantly in their Extraversion scores as their mean difference is not significant.
12. The Science and Arts group student teachers do not differ significantly in their Neuroticism scores.
13. The Science and Arts group student teachers do not differ significantly in their Extraversion scores.
14. The Undergraduate and Postgraduate students do not differ significantly in their Neuroticism scores.
15. The Undergraduate and Postgraduate students do not differ significantly in their Extraversion scores.
16. There is no significant difference between the mean scores of Neuroticism scores of student teachers who have teaching experience and those who do not have teaching experience.
17. There is no significant difference between the mean scores of Extraversion scores of student teachers who have teaching experience and those who do not have teaching experience
18. There is no significant difference between the mean scores of Neuroticism scores of the Urban and Rural student teachers.
19. There is no significant difference between the mean scores of Extraversion scores of the Urban and Rural student teachers.

20. There is no significant mean difference between the student teachers in Neuroticism scores regarding the background variable parental qualifications.
21. There is no significant mean difference between the student teachers in Extraversion scores regarding the background variable parental qualifications.
22. The mean difference is found to be significant. Therefore, the male students and female students differ significantly in their teaching competency.
23. The English medium students and Tamil medium students differ significantly in their teaching competency as their mean difference is found to be significant.
24. There is no significant difference between the mean scores of teaching competency scores of B.Ed. student teachers who had admitted through CENTAC and CET.
25. The Private and Government college students do not differ significantly in their teaching competency as their mean difference is not significant.
26. The Science and Arts students do not differ significantly in their teaching competency.
27. The Undergraduate and Postgraduate students do not differ significantly in their teaching competency
28. There is no significant difference in the mean scores of teaching competency scores of B.Ed. student teachers who have teaching experience and those who do not have teaching experience.
29. The Urban and Rural students do not differ significantly in their teaching competency as their mean difference is not significant.
30. There is no significant mean difference between the students in their teaching competency with regard to the background variable parental qualification.

5.8 **Discussion and Conclusion:**

i) The mean scores of extraversion scores have slight edge over the mean scores of Neuroticism. But the mean scores of extrovert are just above the half of the total scores. Hence as far as the extraversion characteristics, the B.Ed. student teachers are just above average.

ii) The level of teaching competency of B.Ed. student teachers is just above average. They need more practice before they go for intensive teaching practice. Enough time should be given to practice Micro teaching in B.Ed. course.

iii) Extraversion has no relationship with teaching competency. But Neuroticism has relationship with teaching competency. But the relationship is negative. Hence the students who scored more marks in Neuroticism will score less marks in teaching competency and vice versa. To lower neurotic tendency one can undergo relaxation training, desensitizing training, thought stopping etc. which in turn may increase teaching competency. By removing the fear and they should be thorough in their subject that may increase the teaching competency of B.Ed. student teachers.

iv) Sex has influence on B.Ed. student teachers in Neuroticism and teaching competency. But sex has no influence in the case of Extraversion. Female extrovert teachers are better than the male. This is because the female teachers take things seriously and concentrate more on their work.

v) The medium of instruction at school level is found to influence Neuroticism and teaching competency, but not in extraversion students. The English medium and Tamil medium students differ in their personality. Students with Neuroticism studied under English medium school tend to excel their counterpart in personality. Both English medium and Tamil medium students are in average level.

vi) The type of admission does not have influence on Neuroticism, Extraversion and Teaching Competency of the B.Ed. student teachers. Teaching competency and personality does not depend on the type of admission. Both the CENTAC and CET students are in average level in their teaching competency.

vii) Type of college does not have influence on Neuroticism, Extraversion and Teaching Competency of the B.Ed. student teachers. The Private and Government College students do not show any significant difference in their personality but they differ in their teaching competency. Normally the Private colleges provide a congenial atmosphere to the students to enrich their skills and abilities but they have not made any influence on their personality.

viii) Subject specialization has no influence on Neuroticism, Extraversion and Teaching Competency of the B.Ed. student teachers. But the Extrovert Science students are better than the Arts students in their personality and teaching competency. This shows that the specialization of Science group helps the individual to improve their personality and teaching competency.

ix) Educational qualification of the B.Ed. students has no influence on Neuroticism, Extraversion and Teaching Competency. The postgraduates excel the Undergraduates in their personality and teaching competency .Higher degree has influence on teaching competency. it is because they would have thorough knowledge and participated in several symposium and seminars.

x) Teaching experience has no influence on Neuroticism, Extraversion and Teaching Competency of B.Ed. student teachers. But it is found that the experienced extraversion student teachers are better than the inexperienced student teachers.

xi) Locality of the residence has no influence on Neuroticism, Extraversion and Teaching Competency of B.Ed. student teachers. The students from urban area show slight difference in their teaching competency than the rural area students. It may be because; the urban students have better facilities than the rural students.

xii) The parental qualification has no influence on Neuroticism, Extraversion and Teaching Competency of B.Ed. student teachers.

5.7 Recommendations:

1) In order to enhance the teaching competency of student teachers, the training college and the institution may think to revitalize teacher education programme.
2) Yoga and meditation can be included in the curriculum to enhance the personality of the students.
3) Personality development programmes can be conducted.
4) Brainstorming session on the topic prescribed may be conducted periodically.
5) Small group discussion techniques can be employed in teaching for B.Ed. student-teachers.
6) The student-teachers should be motivated and instructed to read many books in relation to all fields to develop their personality and teaching competency.
7) The student-teachers should be asked to enrich themselves about the present trend, recent inventions and technologies to be a competent teacher.

8) The student-teachers should learn to use Internet in positive manner which provides them a wide knowledge about everything in the world to develop their personality and to become a competent teacher.

9) The student-teachers should be encourages to exhibit their novel thoughts and ideas and should be given enough chance to develop them.

10) Experts in education can be invited to give a lecture on Micro teaching simulated teaching.

11) Students must be encouraged to improve their personality characteristics.

12) Enough time should be given to practice Micro teaching in B.Ed. course.

5.7 Suggestion for Further Research:

- A correlation study of the Personality and teaching competency of D.T.Ed. Students can be undertaken.
- Personality in relation to academic achievement of the college students can be studied.
- A study on Personality, Self efficacy and Teaching Competency can be undertaken.
- The role of Personality in predicting the Teaching competency of M.Ed. students. A longitudinal study can be undertaken.
- Studies may be conducted to find out the influence of other personality characteristics like Psychoticism, introversion on teaching competency.
- Studies may be taken up on the psychological variables of teachers in enhancing the teaching.
- The study with wide range area of sample can be done.
- A Correlational study can be conducted on Personality and Teaching competency of school teachers.
- Personality and Teaching competency of teacher educators can be studied.

BIBLIOGRAPHY

Books:

1) Afifi, A.A & Azen, S.P. (1972). Statistical Analysis: A computer oriented approach. New York: Academic Press.
2) Bernard, H.W. (1965). Psychology of learning and teaching. New York: Mc Graw –Hill Book Company.
3) Coleman, J.C.(1960).Personality dynamics and effective behaviour . U.S.A: Scott, Foreskman and co.
4) Crow, L.P. and Crow, A (1973). Educational Psychology. New Delhi: Eurasia Publishing House.
5) Dandapani, S. (2000). Advanced Educational Psychology. New Delhi: Anmol Publication Pvt. Ltd.
6) David, F (1986). Psychology for teachers. London: the British psychological Society and Mc Milan Publishers Pvt. Ltd.
7) Frank.S. Freeman, (1962.) Theory and practice of psychological Testing, Oxford & IBH publishing co, New Delhi,
8) Garret, N.E. (1981). Statistics in psychology and Education. Bombay: Vakils, Feffer and Simons Ltd.
9) Khanna. S,D. T.P. Lamba, V.A. Sexena, Murthy. V,(1989).Education in the emerging Indian Society. Doaba House, Delhi,
10) Kuppuswamy. B. (1993) Advanced Educational Psychology. Sterling Publishers. New Delhi.
11) Larry. A. Hjelle and Daniel. J. Ziegler, Personality Theories, McGraw Hill Book Co, Singapore.
12) Mangal. S.K,(1994) Advanced Educational Psychology, Prentice Hall, New Delhi.
13) Ponnaian. M, Syce Aroquiasamy, Panch Ramalingam,(2000) The concise Dictionary of Education, PR Books, Delhi.

14) Premnath,(1979) The Bases of Education, S. Chand & Company Ltd, New Delhi,
15) Sharma. R.A,(1995) Fundamentals of Educational Research, International Publishing house, Meerut.
16) Taneja. V.R,(1989) Educational thought and practice, Serling Publishers, New Delhi,

Journals:

i) Amaladoss, S.X (2005). Teaching Competency and its dimension in post Graduate. Chemistry. Tr. A Cor. Rl. study. Research & Reflections on Education Vol. 36, 10-16.
ii) Arora. R.K,(1985) Personality Constituents and their relation A study of inter correlation ship, Indian Journal of Applied Psychology, Vol 22(1) PP 46-52
iii) Betty. T. Haslett (1976). Dominions of Teaching Effectiveness: A student perceptive. The Journal of Experimental Education, 1414, 4-10.
iv) David E. Hunt,(1967),Teacher Trainee Personality and Initial Teaching Style American Educational Research Journal, Vol. 4, No. 3,p.253-259. Jeba. A (2005). Teaching Competency and mental health of student teachers in a District Institute of Education and Training (DIET). Experiments in Education, Vol. XXXIII Chennai, January 2005.
v) Kothari - R.G and shah. A.H. (1997) Teacher education at Secondary level. Some observation, New Frontiers in Education, Vol XXVII, No.3.
vi) Prahallada, N.N (2004). Teachers as inspiring agents. Edu Tracks, 39, 19-24.
vii) Vasanthi, R and Anandhi, E (1997). Factors affecting Teacher Effectiveness of B.Ed. Student Teachers. The progress of Education, 71 (6), 137-140.

viii) Singh D; Choudhury DR; Rao N P; Nayar S,(1990)Personality characteristic of teachers involved in the delivery of primary health care (Sevagram Experiment) Indian Journal of Community Medicine.; 15(3): 121-6.

ix) Wadhwa. B.S,(1987) Personality and attitude measures of convent school teachers in relation to Religion, Religious Fundamentalism and subject, Indian Journal of applied Psychology, Vo1.24 (2) 107.

Abstracts:

1. Avery, R. E. (1985). An assessment of the relationship between teacher, teaching style, student learning style, and the academic achievement of twelfth grade students (Doctoral dissertation, University of Massachusetts). Dissertation Abst. International &, 12A.
2. Barto, Valerie, A, (1998) The relationship between personality traits of selected New Jersey public high school educators successful and academic achievement of at risk students, Seton Hall University, College of Education and Human Service, Dissertation Abstracts International Vol 59, No. 1015
3. Carlyn, M. (1976). The relationship between Myers-Briggs personality characteristics and teaching preferences of prospective teachers. Doctoral dissertation, Michigan State University.
4. Cutchin, Gregory Cahrles,(1999) Relationships between the big five personality factors and performance criteria for in service high school teachers, Purdue University, Dissertation Abstracts International Vol 59. No.7, 2263.
5. DeNovellis, R., & Lawrence, G. (1983). Correlates of teacher personality variables (Myers-Briggs) and classroom observation data. Research in 6, 37-46.

6. Eysenck, Sybil, Kozeny & Jeri,(1991) Cross Cultural comparisons of personality; Czech and English subjects. Psychological Abstracts; Vol 78, No.9, Page.I521
7. Eysenck S.B.G, Eysenck, H.J and Barrett. (1991)Personality and Individual Differences. Psychological Abstracts Vol. 6.N o.1,.21-29
8. Grace Annie Mathews, (1997). Principles of teaching profession New Frontiers in Education Vol XXVII, No. 4,
9. Raiszadesh, Azar. 0,(1999) Relationship between personality type, learning style preference and mathematics achievement in College developmental mathematics, The University of Termessee. Dissertation Abstracts International Vol 59, No.7, 2407

Survey:

Prakasham, D (1986). Study on Teacher effectiveness as a function of school organizational climate and Teaching Competency. Fourth Survey of Educational Research, NCERT 2, 1036.

Articles:

i) Bhosale, R.A.(2005). Local wisdom - qualitative improvement in teacher training programme. Edutracks, 46, 23-27.
ii) Pramela, A.(2002) teacher education –current issues and restructuring measures , Edutracks,34,23-25.
iii) Prameela, N.N.(2004) Teachers as inspiring agents. Edutracks, 39, 19-24.
iv) Usha Devi, P.,(2002). Qualitative improvement of teacher education, Edutracks. 36, 22-25
v) Vasanthi, R. and Anandhi, E.(1997) Factors affecting teacher effectiveness of B.Ed., student teachers. The progress of education, 71,(6),137-140.
vi) Viswanathappa, G.(2005) Attitude towards teaching and teaching competency . Edutracks, 8, 21-27.

PERSONALITY AND TEACHING COMPETENCY OF B.ED.STUDENT TEACHERS

Author

Dr. B. ANBOUCARASSY

Laxmi Book Publication

Price: /-

Personality and Teaching Competency of B.Ed. Student Teachers

Dr. B. Anboucarassy

ISBN:

Published by,
Lulu Publication
3101 Hillsborough St,
Raleigh, NC 27607,
United States.

Printed by,
Laxmi Book Publication,
258/34, Raviwar Peth,
Solapur, Maharashtra, India.
Contact No. : +91 9595 359 435
Website: http://www.isrj.org
Email ID: ayisrj@yahoo.in

ACKNOWLEDGEMENT

I am very happy to express my gratitude to the lord almighty that showered His grace upon me, especially in the course of my research.

I owe my sincere gratitude to my research guide Dr. R. John Louis Manoharan, Selection Grade Lecturer in Education, Department of Education, Pope John Paul college of Education, Puducherry, for his extraordinary helping nature, unfailing guidance, and magnanimous support throughout the course of my work. I am also indebted to him for his timely valuable suggestions, which helped me enormously to carry this work successfully.

I sincerely thank the Department of Education, Alagappa University, Karaikudi, for their cooperation in my endurance to complete this study successfully

I wish to express my sincere gratitude to Sr. Philomine Mary, Principal, Immaculate college of Education, Tagore Nagar, Puducherry, whose kind office permitted and encouraged me to complete the present study.

I express my sincere thanks to all my colleagues of Immaculate College of Education, Tagore Nagar, Puducherry, for their valuable suggestions and support throughout the course of my research work.

I thank sincerely to Sr. Philomine Mary, Principal, Immaculate college of Education, Tagore Nagar, Puducherry, Mr. Thomas, Principal of Loyola college of Education, Koodampakkam, Puducherry, Dr. Pakkirisammy, Principal, Correspondent Dr. Gunasekaran, Venketeshwara College of Education, Puducherry, for allowing me to collect the data from student teachers. I express my gratitude to Mr. J.A. Ebenezer, Lecturer Pope John Paul II College of Education, and

Puducherry for his kind nature and valuable advice throughout the course of my research.

I owe special debt of gratitude to Mrs. Guna, Librarian, Immaculate college of Education, Tagore Nagar, Puducherry; who helped in this endeavor.

I thank all the B.Ed. Teacher Trainees (2006-2007) of Immaculate College of Education, Loyola college of Education and Venketeshwara College of Education, who participated as respondents in this research programme.

I thank my brother Dr. B. Mohan Kumar, for his encouragement and support given in publishing this book. Last but not least I am very grateful to my husband Dr. Praveen Kumar Cyril. K, Lecturer , Bharathidasan Govt. College for Women, (Autonomous) Puducherry, who has been grater inspiration, encouragement which made scholarly work easier and more fulfilling, without which my study would not have completed on time.

- **Dr. B. ANBOUCARASSY**

PREFACE

Healthy development of the individual and his personality may be regarded as one of the aims of education. Education has to be arranged that it helps the process of personality development. It is well know that teaching is influenced by personality characteristics of teacher. In the words of secondary education commission (1952-53), every teacher and educationalist of experiences knows that even the best curriculum and the perfect syllabus remains dead, unless quickened in to life by right methods of teaching and right kind of teachers. However good may be the system of education, curriculum and textbooks if the teachers are not efficient, competent and if the teachers are not well balanced in their personality then education by and large will be ineffective. Teachers play an important role in the academic achievement of pupils. It is the responsibility of the teacher to make the pupils to grow in the full status in the overall development. Teacher should provide the necessary experiences and training to the pupil and ensure them to behave as per the expectations of society and lead a successful life. In order to succeed in such duties the teacher should be more efficient and alert.

The student teachers are at the threshold of entering into the career of teaching. Personality plays an important role in teaching profession. A student teacher should have good personality charters in the midst of hectic life prevailing in the modern world. The future of a nation depends upon the role played by the members of the teaching community. It is a pleasant privilege of the teacher, to shape the children of the nation into useful citizens of tomorrow. Therefore personality and teaching competency of the student teacher should be developed to face the growing, which in turn enhance their teaching performance.

By considering this in mind, the author explores the level of personality characteristics and teaching competency of the student teachers. Present work is an attempt to find out the inner relationship among personality and teaching competency of B.Ed., student teachers. Definitely this work will lead to better understanding of the proper conditions for the maintenance of the good personality and teaching competency of the student teachers.

- Dr. B. Anboucarassy

CONTENT

LIST OF TABLES

www.ingramcontent.com/pod-product-compliance
Ingram Content Group UK Ltd.
Pitfield, Milton Keynes, MK11 3LW, UK
UKHW041937190726
13854UKWH00004B/1632